The
Round-the-World
Cook Book

BY

IDA BAILEY ALLEN

PUBLISHED BY THE BEST FOODS, INC.

MAKERS OF

NUCOA
THE DOUBLE-PURPOSE FOOD

Printed in the United States of America by
J. J. LITTLE AND IVES COMPANY, NEW YORK

INTRODUCTION

Adventures on the High Seas
of Cookery

MANY months have passed since Franz, the International Chef, and I set forth on an adventure. Through storm and calm, we have sailed the High Seas of Cookery, nosing our vessel's prow into the culinary ports of the world.

Our staunch ship was a testing kitchen; the engine room was the kitchen range; our rigging consisted of spoons, bowls, pots and pans. The worthy crew were dietitians and kitchen aids. The Captain was Franz, the International Chef; our passengers were the tasters and testers who day after day scrambled up the gangplank and into the galley.

I mapped the course of the expedition, and piloted the Good Ship, which sailed away under the flag of The Best Foods, Inc., in search of the world's choicest recipes.

World Is Kin on Food

Famous folk from near and far heard rumors of our good ship, and hastened to come aboard,—noted gourmets, captains of industry, women of foreign lands, famous musicians, polished diplomats and consul-generals, and eager homemakers from Texas to Maine. They tasted and sipped and gave their unstinted praise,—and then, they ate it all up! The whole world, we found, could get together on one subject—food.

Up through the dark rivers of Russia, along the ports of the blue Mediterranean, into the icy fjords of Norway, to far-away China and Japan, to sunny India and the Arabian desert, we ventured, coming at last to the rivers and lakes of our own land. We found many strange dishes, some too exotic for our American palates, but the best of them, simple, delicious and economical. And to the surprise of Captain and Crew alike, some of the most interesting of all were those of our own America.

So, here in the Ship's Log, we have written the record of our adventures and discoveries. This is not an encyclopedia—but a brief Guide Book to World Cookery. The recipes have been standardized to American needs with the New Nucoa, the double-purpose food which is not only suitable for every table use but fills five major cooking needs:

A rich shortening for cakes, pies, breads and pastries
A delicious seasoning for vegetables
A basis for sweet and savory sauces, soups and gravies
A basis for candies and icings
A medium for all pan and Simplified French Frying.

There is no other one food that can be so successfully used on the table, where all the family loves it, and for every cooking use as well. And there is no other shortening you could think of using as a spread for bread.

New Nucoa Is Different

Some of you may say that Nucoa is a product familiar to you for many years. This is true, so far as the name Nucoa is concerned. But the New Nucoa is different, better than the Nucoa produced before. It is the result of years of experimentation and many months of practical testing. The New Nucoa has been created to fill the need of every one of you who wishes to secure a wholesome spread and to cook foods of perfect flavor economically and with one and the same product.

The New Nucoa is so inexpensive that you can afford to use it as a shortening, a frying medium and a seasoning—in brief, for every cooking need. It is so nutritious that you can with assurance spread it generously on bread for your children.

The New Nucoa is of unqualified purity, easily digested, as high in energy value as any spread that may be obtained, wholesome and delicious. It is truly fresh. As soon as it is made it is rushed to the stores by The Best Foods trucks, ready to be transferred to the table for use as a spread and to enrich and make more wholesome and delicious the foods you cook at a price you can afford.

The New Nucoa has been approved by the American Medical Association and the Good Housekeeping Bureau.

The New Nucoa is delicious for all table purposes. As a spread for bread, hot toast or biscuits, griddle cakes and waffles, it graces the finest meal. Even the Suzette Sauce for Crêpes Suzette—the most delectable of French desserts calling for a spread—is perfect when made with Nucoa. When used as a spread, the New Nucoa may be quickly transformed to a golden yellow color by using the color wafer (approved by the U. S. Government) that is inclosed with every package.

For cooking purposes the New Nucoa may be used as it comes—milky white—or it may be tinted yellow, according to preference. There is no department of cooking in which the New Nucoa cannot be used with ease and perfect results.

The All-Purpose Food

Its smooth plastic texture makes it especially easy to use in mixing hot breads, cookies and all pastries in less time.

It is a perfect medium for pan and for Simplified French Frying—the odor is almost indiscernible and the fried foods do not stick or have an oily or greasy taste. Furthermore, foods fried in it are highly digestible.

The New Nucoa can be used freely, without fear of extravagance, in seasoning vegetables and in cooking eggs, processes that formerly called for the most expensive spreads.

During our tour of Food discoveries, I have subjected the New Nucoa in the experimental kitchen to every possible table and cooking test. I find that in comparison with other spreads it comes first because of its uniformity of flavor and its economy. In comparison with other shortenings the New Nucoa leads in flavor and in ease of use (plasticity). It is outstanding because it is an all-purpose shortening. It is the food contribution of the decade to economical and healthful living.

I hope this little book will start you off on your own Tour of Discovery, and that, with us, you will enjoy the foods of America and the Lands-Around-The-World.

Ida Bailey Allen

To the Ladies

I T HAS been a great pleasure and privilege for me to assist Mrs. Allen in the practical preparation of this little book.

As a chef, I have been astounded by the wonderful American food discovery—the New Nucoa. Whether I have used it for a delicate sauce or for baking or frying, or as a simple spread on breads or biscuits, I have found the New Nucoa to be absolutely dependable in quality and taste, and—what is so important to everyone—whether European or American, Nucoa is most economical.

Not only can the New Nucoa be used in simple dishes, but it is suitable as an ingredient in the most refined examples of the culinary art.

Franz

TABLE OF CONTENTS

HOW TO USE THESE RECIPES

How to Measure

All the recipes in this book have been standardized for the use of level measurements.

The necessary utensils include two standard half-pint glass or aluminum cups, marked into halves, quarters and thirds; and a set of measuring spoons or several standard tablespoons and teaspoons.

To measure Nucoa pack it down and level it off with a knife. To measure a portion of a cupful follow the numbers on the measuring cup. To measure a half spoonful, fill the spoon with Nucoa, pack it down, level it off with a knife and divide it in halves lengthwise.

If Nucoa is to be melted before measuring, this is indicated in the recipe.

To measure any dry ingredient heap the utensil with it and then level off with a knife. Sift flour before measuring. In measuring do not pack down the ingredient. To measure a portion of a cupful, follow the numbers on the measuring cup. To measure a half spoonful, fill the spoon with the ingredient, level it off with a knife and divide in halves lengthwise. To measure a fourth teaspoonful, divide a half spoonful.

How Many the Recipes Serve

Unless otherwise specified the recipes in this book are proportioned to serve six.

When to Color Nucoa

Nucoa may be used milky white just as it comes from the package in preparing almost all the dishes given in this book. However, in making Hard or Maître d'Hôtel Sauce, in preparing toast or sandwiches, and in seasoning vegetables it is advisable to tint it golden to insure the accustomed color. Nucoa should also be tinted golden for all table use.

9

How to Tint Nucoa Golden

It takes but a few minutes to color Nucoa. Place Nucoa in a bowl and allow it to soften at room temperature. Tear the color wafer in half. Hold each vertically, and tap gently, spreading the powder over the Nucoa. (If a light yellow tint is desired, one-half the contents of the color wafer will be found sufficient.) Scrape and work color into top layer of Nucoa with a table knife or spatula until you have an even color. Then break up the pound and mix evenly throughout, using a fork or other suitable utensil. Work the color through the Nucoa until the tint is uniform. Pack in a crock or glass bowl and keep in a cool place. This color complies with the pure food requirements of the United States Department of Agriculture.

SOUPS

La soupe! La soupe! It's the supper call of all France.

Translated into Swedish, Dutch, Russian or Arabic, it is heard 'round the world.

For soup—thick, nourishing, savory soup is the everyday food wherever people live and work.

And here we've gathered them for you—rich, delicious, penny-saving soups from the Italian campagna, the Austrian Alps, the Swedish fjords, the English downs, and the hills and plains of our America.

Serve them, as the main course at lunch or dinner, in bright colorful peasant bowls. Or bear them to the table, hot and steaming, in huge tureens of honorable ancestry, with garnishes of croutons, or with baskets of brown crusty bread or rolls. Or add a real home touch to your international cookery, and serve hot crumbly cornbread or flaky biscuits, split and spread with the New Nucoa.

ALL MEASUREMENTS ARE LEVEL

French Onion Soup

3 tablespoons Nucoa	1 teaspoon salt
3 cups thinly sliced onions	1/8 teaspoon pepper
1/4 teaspoon sugar	6 rounds of toast, spread with Nucoa
1 1/2 quarts soup stock	Grated Parmesan cheese

Melt the Nucoa; add the onions; and sauté until yellow. Add the sugar and when caramelized the soup stock, salt and pepper. Simmer until the onions are soft. Transfer to six individual soup bowls; and top each with a round of toast spread with Nucoa. Place under the broiler flame or in a very hot oven until the toast browns. Serve with Parmesan cheese.

Swedish Chopped Vegetable Cream Broth

1/2 cup finely shredded raw parsnip	1 teaspoon very finely minced onion
1/3 cup finely shredded white turnip	2 tablespoons Nucoa
1/2 cup finely shredded carrot	1 quart milk
3/4 cup finely shredded celery	1/2 teaspoon salt
	1/8 teaspoon pepper

11

Place the prepared vegetables in a saucepan and pour in enough boiling water to barely cover the bottom. Add the Nucoa; put on the lid and cook the vegetables until tender, so slowly that they will merely steam, about twenty five minutes. In the meantime, scald the milk. When the vegetables are tender, pour in the scalded milk; add the seasonings; let stand where the broth will keep hot for ten minutes and serve. (Do not boil.)

Gardener's Wife Soup

1¾ cups finely chopped cabbage	1 medium-sized carrot, shredded
1 small head lettuce, shredded	1 quart cold water
1 good-sized beet, peeled and shredded	1 teaspoon salt
½ cup finely diced turnip	⅛ teaspoon pepper
1¼ cups chopped potatoes	1 teaspoon sugar
¾ cup minced celery	1½ tablespoons Nucoa
1 cup fresh or canned peas	1 quart soup stock

Grated cheese

Combine the vegetables; add the cold water, salt, pepper, sugar and Nucoa. Cover. Bring to a boil and boil thirty-five minutes or until the vegetables are tender. Add the stock, which should be heated, and continue cooking slowly. Uncover for twenty minutes. Serve with croutons and grated American or Parmesan cheese or with toast spread lightly with Nucoa, sprinkled with cheese and browned in the oven.

Queen Victoria's Favorite Soup

1 cup minced cold chicken	1 tablespoon Nucoa
1 quart chicken stock	1 tablespoon flour
1 cup top cream	2 hard-cooked egg yolks

Salt

Add the chicken to the broth and heat. Stir in the top cream and when boiling thicken with the egg yolks, mashed with the Nucoa and flour. Season to taste. Cook and stir until creamy. Serve plain or sprinkled with a little minced parsley.

Lentil Soup

⅔ cup green lentils	1½ teaspoons salt
3 tablespoons Nucoa	⅛ teaspoon pepper
¼ cup minced onion	6 cups boiling water
1 cup chopped celery leaves (optional)	2 cups milk
½ tablespoon sugar	3 tablespoons flour

Let the lentils stand over night in cold water to cover. Drain thoroughly. Melt the Nucoa in a medium-sized kettle; add the onion and celery leaves and sauté slowly five minutes. Add the lentils, seasonings and the boiling water. Cover closely and simmer two hours, or until the lentils are soft. Then rub the lentils and liquid together through a sieve. Return to the kettle; add the milk; bring to boiling point and thicken with the flour, stirred smooth with an extra three tablespoons milk. Serve with croutons or with thin slices of frankfurter stirred into the soup.

Maine Fish Chowder

1½ pounds cod, haddock or any other white flesh fish	1 teaspoon salt
	¼ teaspoon pepper
3 tablespoons Nucoa	1 pint sliced potatoes
¼ cup sliced onion	1 pint rich milk
1 quart boiling water	4 tablespoons flour

Remove the skin and bones from the fish and cut it in medium-sized cubes. Melt the Nucoa in a heavy kettle; add the onion and cook slowly until yellowed. Pour in the boiling water and add the fish. Cover and simmer for twenty minutes; then add the seasonings and potatoes and cook until they are tender, about twenty minutes longer. Add the milk; bring to boiling point and stir in the flour, blended with an extra tablespoon of Nucoa. Cook and stir until slightly thickened. Serve in bowls or big plates with pilot crackers as an accompaniment.

Italian Steamed Clam Soup

1½ tablespoons Nucoa	3 medium-sized tomatoes
2 cloves garlic, shredded, or	3 cups boiling water
	⅛ teaspoon pepper
¼ cup minced onion	36 hard-shell clams

Melt the Nucoa in a good-sized kettle and slowly cook the garlic or onion in it until yellowed. Peel the tomatoes and cut in small dice. Add to the Nucoa; pour in the water and add the pepper. Be sure the clams are thoroughly washed and free from sand. Place in a sieve or colander that will fit into the kettle but that will not quite touch the surface of the water. Cover very tightly and place over a very low heat; steam for an hour and a half. Serve six clams to a person in large soup plates with the soup poured over and around.

Constantinople Pepper-Pot

½ cup cow-peas
1½ quarts well-seasoned soup stock
¾ pound fresh or pickled tripe, cut in small dice
Juice ½ lemon
Salt
Pepper

1 clove garlic, crushed, or 2 tablespoons minced onion
½ tablespoon flour
1 tablespoon Nucoa
1 egg
Boiled rice

Soak the cow-peas overnight. Drain and add to the stock, which should be boiling. Cook rapidly for an hour. In the meantime, cover the tripe with cold water and bring to boiling point. Then scrape it and cut in narrow inch lengths or cubes. Add the tripe and garlic to the stock, replenishing the stock as it evaporates. Simmer two hours. Season to taste with salt and pepper. Cream together the Nucoa, flour and lemon juice. Stir carefully into the soup and boil a minute or two, stirring constantly. Add the egg, beaten light and mixed with a little of the hot soup. Reheat and serve at once with large spoonsful of boiled rice in the center of each plate.

TOASTS

Who invented toast? Nobody knows. But America has discovered the various new uses and possibilities of Toast: Toast for breakfast, of course! Toast at teatime, certainly! Toast made in the kitchen over burning coals, or piping hot at the table from the latest electric toaster.

But are you missing some of the smartest newest ways of using toast?

Take the savory toasts, for instance. Cheese deliciously melted on dainty toast squares, nuts crisply browned or bits of anchovy on toast rounds and diamonds, and served hot with salad, or soup, or as a snack.

Or sautéd toast points as garnishes with creamed eggs, or chicken à la king.

Or consider canapés . . . the smartest appetizers that the most knowing hostesses are serving with cold drinks, or as a first course at lunch or dinner. Toast, sautéd or from a toaster, in fancy shapes, garnished with chopped egg yolks, pimiento stars, borders of caviar or fish paste, or cream cheese moistened with onion juice. Keep them finger-dainty when served in the living room—larger and more elaborate when served at table with a fork.

Or the sweet toasts . . . Cinnamon toast with afternoon tea, or with chocolate on a snappy night, or as a simple dessert at lunch. Or delicate French toast, the 'lost bread' of French children. Dipped in uncooked, unsweetened custard and sautéd, it's a versatile dish, delicious at breakfast, smart at lunch as a savory, or as a sweet.

But whatever the toast, there is one best spread that may be generously used. If toast is sautéd, there's only one frying medium that insures deliciousness without burning. The New Nucoa is the answer to both. Make it golden for table use, in accordance with the directions in the package, chill and shape into dainty pats, balls or cubes.

ALL MEASUREMENTS ARE LEVEL

Savory Toasts or Canapés

1. Make a paste of six medium-sized minced sardines, one mashed hard-cooked egg, one-half minced pimiento, one tablespoon lemon juice and one tablespoon Nucoa, colored golden. Season with salt and paprika. Serve on small strips of hot toast.

2. Scramble together three eggs, one-half cup minced ham, one-fourth teaspoon mustard, one-fourth teaspoon each paprika and salt, and one tablespoon Nucoa. Serve on small thin rounds of bread fried in Nucoa.

3. Melt one tablespoon Nucoa; add one-half cup minced canned shrimps, one-half tablespoon anchovy paste, two beaten eggs, one tablespoon milk, and salt and paprika to taste. Scramble over a low heat; and serve on small squares of hot toast spread with Nucoa, colored golden.

Bread Croutons for Soup

These may be baked or toasted. In any case, cut white bread one-fourth inch thick and spread it thickly on both sides with the Nucoa. Cut in dice; place in a pan thickly rubbed with Nucoa and bake in the oven, or toast on a broiler, stirring occasionally so the croutons will be evenly browned.

Cinnamon Toast

Sliced white bread	Sifted powdered sugar
Nucoa	Cinnamon

The bread should be sliced one-fourth inch thick. Toast on both sides; spread generously with Nucoa, colored golden, way to the edges; cover with the sugar, mixed with the cinnamon in the proportion of two teaspoons cinnamon to a cup of sugar. Pile up and place in the oven for a few moments so the sugar and Nucoa will blend.

French Toast

12 slices white bread, cut one-fourth inch thick and halved	1 teaspoon sugar
	1/3 teaspoon baking powder
1 egg, slightly beaten	1 pint milk
Few grains salt	Nucoa

Beat the egg; add the salt, sugar, baking powder and milk. Dip the bread in this and let stand a minute. In the meantime, melt enough Nucoa in the bottom of a good-sized frying pan to barely cover. Drain the bread a second, place in the frying pan and brown slowly, first on one side then the other.

Serve plain as a savory with crisp bacon or frizzled ham, or serve as a sweet with syrup, honey, jam or jelly; with sifted powdered sugar and cinnamon, or with sliced sugared peaches, with warmed stewed prunes, or with dried apricots.

FRYING

The verb to fry has two meanings: To cook in a pan or on a griddle in heated fat of any kind. This is called pan frying or sautéing. To cook in very hot fat, sufficient in quantity to completely submerge the food. This is called French frying.

Pan Frying or Sautéing

This method is most often used in browning cooked foods, as sliced potatoes, or in frying thin raw foods as minute steak, very thin slices of veal cutlet, or small fish, eggplant or summer squash; in frying eggs and omelettes, in cooking griddle cakes or French toast, and in preparing thin fritters.

Every woman who has cooked at all is familiar with pan frying. She may not, however, be familiar with pan frying with the New Nucoa. The method to be followed is the same as that generally used with but this exception. Try to use a heavy frying pan through which the heat comes slowly and evenly, so that the flavors of the cooking food may be fully developed. Then, the New Nucoa itself, which is delicate and nutritive in quality because it is made of the best fresh vegetable oils blended with whole milk, will not be subjected to too high a temperature. Thus it can contribute all its valuable nutritive qualities. Every woman knows that plain milk should not be overcooked. The same general principle applies to the New Nucoa, because of the milk it contains. The white flecks that you will see appearing in a frying pan in which the New Nucoa is cooking is proof positive of the presence of milk, for they consist of milk solids, known technically as casein. In frying, these milk solids are absorbed by the sautéing or frying food and help to make them more healthful and delicious.

Simplified French Frying

French frying has been used for many years in the frying of raw foods, such as potatoes, small fish and croquettes as well as fritters, crullers and other batters of fairly thick consistency. But, up to now it has been a troublesome and expensive process, calling for a special

17

frying kettle and frying basket and two or three pounds of fat for the frying. The expense, together with the necessity for the use of a frying thermometer or the old cube of bread test for gauging the temperature of the fat, the indigestibility of the foods, cooked in overhot fat, and the unpleasant odors of smoking fat that resulted during the frying process, prevented many from preparing the French fried potatoes and fish croquettes, fritters and crullers that properly cooked are delicious.

With the discovery of the New Nucoa has come a new method of French frying—a simplified method—that does not call for special equipment or for the use of pounds of Nucoa. A method that eliminates practically all frying odors and that produces digestible foods. A heavy frying pan is the only utensil required and only enough Nucoa is required to *barely float the food*. The temperature required is much lower than that usually used for deep-fat frying, for foods can be fried in the New Nucoa at a much lower heat; this makes them more digestible. When done, the foods cooked by this Simplified French Frying Method in Nucoa have a tender, delicate crust, with a rich flavor that can be obtained with the use of no other ingredient. The foods are free of grease; they are more digestible because of the dainty crust that cooks on them because of the milk solids contained in the New Nucoa—a crust that helps to keep the fat from penetrating the foods. It is because the fat does not soak into the foods that the New Nucoa goes farther than other fats and proves more economical.

When To Use Simplified French Frying (*with Nucoa*)

In French frying white or sweet potatoes, eggplant, etc.

In French frying croquettes

In French frying fritters of all kinds

In French frying small crullers

In French frying small whole fish, oysters, large clams or fresh shrimps.

Amounts of New Nucoa to be Used in Simplified French Frying for Six People

For quick French fried potatoes, eggplant, sliced onions, shrimps, clams, oysters, small fish and thin fritters, use one-half pound New Nucoa, or enough to give a depth of one-half inch in the pan, when melted.

For crullers, thicker fritters, croquettes and fish cakes, use three-quarters pound New Nucoa or enough Nucoa to give a depth of a scant three-quarters of an inch in the pan, when melted.

In no case should a larger amount of Nucoa be used than that designated, as when this is done the excess casein fries on the bottom of the pan: The low frying temperatures must be observed.

Method

Warm a ten-inch heavy iron frying pan. Into it put the designated quantity of the New Nucoa. Draw the frying pan *off the heat* and place it where the Nucoa will *melt but not burn. When melted,* place the pan over a *slow* heat. If using a gas range or a hot open flame, place an asbestos mat under the frying pan. When the Nucoa bubbles hard and white flecks of milk casein appear on top, put in the prepared food; stir the Nucoa occasionally and slightly. Most of the flecks soon cling to the food, helping to form a fat-proof coating and contributing a more delicious flavor. The fresh American vegetable oils which are present in the Nucoa fry the food. Keep the heat low so the Nucoa cannot smoke or burn; the actual temperature should be under 300 degrees F. Fry the food until golden brown on one side; then turn to brown the other. This process takes longer than the usual deep frying in smoking fat because of the lower temperature employed, but it is not necessary to give close attention to the cooking food during this time except to be sure the Nucoa does not become too hot. If necessary, add a little more Nucoa from time to time, from the edge of the pan. Be careful not to use too much. The food should merely float and not touch the bottom of the pan.

Drain the fried foods on crumpled paper towels or brown paper. *Do not salt potatoes* after frying as the salt present in the Nucoa is sufficient. The New Nucoa is already seasoned.

Croquette Preparation

The croquette mixture should be made as usual. The meat or fish is properly seasoned and put together in the proportion of two and one-half cups of finely minced meat or fish to one-half cup of Thick White Cream Sauce as given in this book. The mixture is chilled. Then it is ready to shape into croquettes from an inch to an inch and a half in thickness. Allowing a tablespoon for each croquette, shape with floured hands into flat croquettes or cutlets; dip in flour; then in an egg slightly beaten with two tablespoons of milk. Coat each croquette with fine dry bread crumbs and cook as directed by the Simplified French Frying Method just discussed.

Care of the Remaining Nucoa

After frying, the remaining Nucoa may be strained through a fine wire sieve into a bowl and used again. Onions or fish do not leave any flavor in the Nucoa after it has been used for frying them. The same Nucoa may be used later for frying fritters, slices of apple or other delicate foods or it may be used in shortening spice cake, gingerbread or any dark bread calling for melted Nucoa.

ALL MEASUREMENTS ARE LEVEL

Simplified French Fried Potatoes

Wash and peel one good-sized potato for each person. Cut the potatoes in lengthwise strips making sixteen to a potato. Let stand in cold water ten minutes. Drain; dry on a towel; then fry in the Nucoa according to the preceding directions, putting a generous layer in the frying pan. Do not attempt to cook the potatoes too fast. Cook until tender and brown. When done, drain on crumpled paper and serve at once.

Simplified French Fried Sweet Potatoes

Wash and boil medium-sized sweet potatoes for fifteen minutes. Then peel and cut in lengthwise strips as for ordinary French fried potatoes. Cook in Nucoa according to the directions given for Simplified French Frying. Drain on crumpled paper towels.

Simplified French Fried Eggplant or Sliced Summer Squash

Peel the eggplant or squash and cut in slices a quarter of an inch thick. Dust with salt and pepper; dip in flour, then in a slightly beaten egg mixed with two tablespoons of milk. Coat with fine dry bread crumbs and cook in Nucoa according to the preceding Simplified French Frying Method. Drain on crumpled paper and serve.

Simplified French Fried Onion Rings

Peel a large Spanish onion and slice one-quarter of an inch thick. Push each slice apart, forming rings. Dust with salt and pepper. Dip in a slightly beaten egg, mixed with two tablespoons milk. Then dip in fine dry bread crumbs and fry according to the Simplified French Frying Method.

Fritter Batter

1 cup flour	⅔ cup water or milk
¼ teaspoon salt	2 eggs
	1 teaspoon melted Nucoa

Sift the flour and salt together into a bowl, gradually beating in the water or milk with an egg beater. Beat the egg yolks; add to the first mixture and when well-mixed stir in the Nucoa and the egg whites, beaten stiff. Use as a basis for fruit, corn or vegetable fritters.

Apple Fritters

Prepare fritter batter as directed above. Peel and core three apples and cut crosswise in one-quarter inch slices. Dip quickly in and out of the fritter batter and fry at once according to the Simplified French Frying Method described in this section. When golden on one side, turn the fritters to brown the other. Drain the fritters on crumpled paper towels and serve dusted thickly with powdered sugar and cinnamon or with a lemon or other fruit sauce.

Green Corn Fritters

½ cup flour	1 egg
⅛ teaspoon salt	½ teaspoon melted Nucoa
½ teaspoon baking powder	1½ cups raw green corn kernels
⅓ cup water or milk	Nucoa for frying

Sift together the flour, salt and baking powder and using a rotary egg beater, beat in the water or milk. Then add the egg, beaten until light. Stir in the Nucoa and mix well. Add the corn and cook according to the Simplified French Frying Method given in this section, dropping in the fritter mixture by medium-sized tablespoonsful. When browned on one side, turn to brown the other. Allow about ten minutes for the cookery. Then drain on crumpled paper towels and serve plain or New England style with maple syrup.

Crullers

1 egg	½ cup milk
⅓ cup sugar	2¼ cups flour
½ teaspoon nutmeg	¼ teaspoon salt
2 tablespoons Nucoa, melted	3 teaspoons baking powder
Nucoa for frying	

Beat the egg until light; add the sugar, nutmeg and melted Nucoa and beat until blended; pour in the milk. Sift together the dry ingredients and add to the first mixture. Transfer in small quantities to a slightly floured board. Roll to a third-inch in thickness, cut into finger-length strips and twist slightly.

Fry in the Nucoa as follows: Put no more than three-quarters of a pound of Nucoa into a heavy 10-inch frying pan, which has been warmed but is not very hot. Use enough to make a depth of a little more than a half-inch. Set aside until the Nucoa melts. Place it over the heat; add a large peeled potato cut in finger lengths and heat gradually over a very low flame stirring occasionally until the potato begins to brown. Then remove the potato and fry the crullers as usual first on one side, then the other until golden. Drain on crumpled paper towels and dust while hot with powdered sugar, sifted with a little cinnamon, or roll in granulated sugar.

Note: If using a gas stove or any very hot open flame, set the frying pan containing the Nucoa on an asbestos mat to keep the temperature lower than usual.

EGGS

To keep in health, said an old Roman proverb, one must stay at table from eggs to apples. And to make that easy, they devised twenty ways to serve eggs, and so set a style that has endured for two thousand years.

Gourmets of the world look to the humble egg for some of their most cherished dishes. France has her flaky omelettes, Switzerland her shirred eggs. Brillat-Savarin, the great epicure, made his reputation on new-laid eggs scrambled with cheese, and America's ham-and-eggs for early breakfast are famed wherever the American flag flies.

But the clever cook—under any flag—knows that to bring out the bland delicacy of eggs, the right seasonings must be used. Only the most subtle flavors are suitable. That's why prominent chefs are adopting the New Nucoa for seasoning and cooking eggs. They approve its blend of sweet pasteurized milk with fresh vegetable oils. Try Nucoa with egg dishes for breakfast, luncheon or light supper. You, too, will be convinced.

ALL MEASUREMENTS ARE LEVEL

Eggs Portuguese Style

3 medium-sized tomatoes	½ teaspoon salt
1 tablespoon Nucoa	1 teaspoon sugar
1 clove garlic, minced	⅛ teaspoon pepper

5 eggs

Peel the tomatoes and cut or chop them. Melt the Nucoa in a medium-sized heavy frying pan; add the garlic or onion and sauté until yellowed. Then add the tomatoes and seasonings and boil until the tomato is soft and the liquid is almost evaporated, about five minutes. Beat the eggs light; stir them into the heated tomato mixture and continue to cook and stir over a medium heat until the egg is coagulated.

Eggs Fried in Nucoa

Nucoa   Salt
Fresh eggs   White pepper

Melt enough Nucoa in a frying pan to barely cover the bottom. Do not let it burn. When bubbling hard, break in the required number of eggs, without letting them touch each other. Dust sparingly with salt and plentifully with pepper; *fry very slowly.* Baste occasionally with the Nucoa in the pan. When done, they should be translucent, and the edges pale brown. Serve on a large platter with a garnish of parsley.

Eggs Benedict

6 thin trim slices cooked or raw ham   Nucoa
6 slices toast   6 poached eggs
                  Hollandaise Sauce

Broil or sauté the ham in a little Nucoa. Spread the toast with Nucoa, colored golden. Arrange the ham on it. Top each piece with a poached egg and pour over a tablespoon and a half of Hollandaise sauce. Dust each serving with a little paprika and serve with or without a sprig of parsley.

Shirred Eggs Swiss Style

2 tablespoons Nucoa   6 tablespoons top cream
6 large eggs   ½ cup finely chopped Swiss cheese
            Salt and pepper

Rub shirred egg dishes or deep fireproof saucers with Nucoa. Into each break an egg. Pour in the top cream; sprinkle over the cheese. Dust sparingly with salt and plentifully with pepper. Place in a moderately hot oven, 350-375 degrees F., and bake until the eggs are set. Allow from ten to twelve minutes.

Eggs Lyonnaise

6 good-sized eggs   2 tablespoons Nucoa
¾ cup chopped onion   Salt and pepper

Melt the Nucoa in a heavy frying pan and when bubbling, add the onion. Sauté slightly until yellowed. Break in the eggs carefully one at a time. Dust with salt and plentifully with pepper and fry slowly until the eggs are set.

Chinese Scrambled Eggs

5 eggs
½ cup minced cooked chicken,
   pork or ham
½ cup chopped peeled
   mushrooms

1 teaspoon soy sauce or kitchen
   bouquet
¼ teaspoon salt
2 tablespoons meat stock or milk
1½ tablespoons Nucoa

Beat the eggs; and add the other ingredients, except the Nucoa. Melt the Nucoa in a heated pan. Pour in the egg mixture and scramble as usual, scraping up the mixture as fast as it coagulates.

Rolled French Omelette

6 eggs
6 tablespoons hot water
½ teaspoon salt

⅛ teaspoon pepper
⅜ teaspoon baking powder
1 tablespoon Nucoa

Break the eggs into a large bowl and beat with a wire whip until the yolks and whites blend. Add the hot water, salt, pepper and baking powder and blend. In the meantime, melt the Nucoa in a large ten-inch smooth frying pan or omelette pan. Tip the pan so the Nucoa coats the bottom and sides. Pour in the egg mixture and cook over a low heat for about three or four minutes, lifting occasionally with a fork. Cook until the mixture is barely firm. Roll with a fork and transfer to a heated platter. Serve garnished with parsley.

Cheese, Ham or Chicken Omelette

Follow the recipe for Rolled French Omelette. While the mixture is cooking sprinkle the top with one-half cup chopped cheese or finely minced ham or chicken. Roll and serve as directed.

Omelette Aux Fines Herbes

Follow the recipe for Rolled French Omelette. While the mixture is cooking sprinkle with four tablespoons finely minced mixed herbs, such as parsley, thyme, marjoram, etc. Roll and serve as directed.

Swedish Omelette

1 tablespoon flour
½ teaspoon salt
⅛ teaspoon pepper

1 cup milk
4 eggs
1½ tablespoons Nucoa

Combine the flour, salt and pepper; gradually add the milk and mix to a smooth paste. Separate the eggs; beat the yolks until thick and lemon-colored and add the milk mixture. Beat the whites until stiff. Slightly fold the egg whites into the milk and egg yolk mixture, leaving some of the white floating in large pieces. In the meantime, melt the Nucoa in a large smooth frying pan and pour in the egg mixture. Cook over a low heat, lifting occasionally about the edges, until the omelette is cooked through and is brown on the bottom. Place under the broiler or in the oven for a few minutes to set the top. Cut the omelette at right angles to the handle of the pan; fold over and transfer to a heated platter. This omelette can stand for ten minutes in a warm oven before serving.

Spanish Omelette

Follow the recipe for Swedish Omelette. When the omelette is cooked, spread with two-thirds cup Spanish Sauce. Cut and fold over as directed. Transfer to a heated platter; pour a little additional sauce around the omelette and serve garnished with sprigs of watercress.

QUICK BREADS

It's May in England, in the days of Good Queen Bess. The newly married brides, conforming to age-old custom, have tucked their wafer irons under their arms, and are off to make wafers for their mothers.

And that, so they say, is the origin of waffles, as we know them today. Whether that's true or not, hot breads and cakes, baked on griddles or iron, or even in ashes by the roadside, have been famed since the world began. Every race has its own 'biscuit.'

But it took America, with her speed ways, to discover how these Old World yeast breads could be turned out to perfection in double-quick time.

Try one of the many cosmopolitan variations for breakfast, lunch, tea or supper. Keep them small and dainty, as the smartest tea rooms do. Fold them hot in a crisp napkin, and accompany them with plenty of the New Nucoa, colored golden, the only blended spread that is delicious on hot breads. See how Nucoa brings out and accentuates their flakiness and flavor.

The New Nucoa is made of pasteurized whole milk, blended with fresh vegetable oils. It's as economical as it is good.

ALL MEASUREMENTS ARE LEVEL

Baking Powder Biscuits

2 cups flour	½ teaspoon salt
4 teaspoons baking powder	6 tablespoons Nucoa
1 teaspoon sugar	¾ cup milk

Sift the dry ingredients together and with the back and edge of a spoon cut in the Nucoa until the consistency of coarse cornmeal. Moisten with the milk and mix until blended. Transfer to a board dusted with flour and roll or pat to one-fourth inch in thickness. Shape with a small biscuit cutter first dipped in flour and transfer to a shallow pan or baking sheet rubbed with Nucoa. Bake in a very hot oven, 400-425 degrees F. for fifteen minutes, or until puffy and brown.

Taffy Biscuits

Follow the recipe for Baking Powder Biscuits. Turn the dough onto a board and roll into an oblong piece one-third of an inch thick. Cream together one-half cup Nucoa and one cup light brown sugar; spread this over the Baking Powder Biscuit dough, roll up like a jelly roll and cut in slices one inch thick. Place cut side down on Nucoa-d pans and bake in a moderate oven, 350 degrees F. for about twenty-five minutes. Serve hot.

Marmalade Biscuits

Follow the recipe for Baking Powder Biscuits. Roll to a scant fourth-inch in thickness. Shape in three-inch rounds with a biscuit cutter. Place a teaspoon of orange marmalade in the center of each round and fold over pressing the edges together. Transfer to a shallow pan or baking sheet rubbed with Nucoa and bake in a hot oven, 375 degrees F. for twenty minutes, or until brown on top.

Russian Piroushkis

Follow the recipe for Baking Powder Biscuits. Roll to one-eighth inch in thickness. Dot the dough with four tablespoons additional Nucoa; fold over in thirds and press the edges together. Roll to one-fourth inch in thickness and shape in two-inch rounds using a biscuit cutter. Combine one and one-half cups chopped left-over meat with gravy or white cream sauce to moisten and place a tablespoon of the mixture on half of the biscuit rounds. Cover each with a second round of the plain dough, moistening the edges and pressing them lightly together. Transfer to a shallow pan rubbed with Nucoa; and brush the tops with an egg yolk, slightly beaten. Bake in a hot oven, 375 degrees F. for twenty minutes, or until puffy and brown on top. Serve hot, plain or with gravy or cream sauce.

Biscuit Nut Bars

2 cups flour	4 tablespoons Nucoa
4 teaspoons baking powder	¾ cup milk
½ teaspoon salt	2 tablespoons Nucoa (additional)
½ cup finely chopped nutmeats	

Sift the dry ingredients; work in the three tablespoons Nucoa with the back and edge of a spoon until flaky. Add the milk and mix until blended. Toss onto a slightly floured board and pat to an oblong shape, a scant half-inch in thickness. Cream the remaining Nucoa and spread it on the mixture. Sprinkle thickly with the nuts. Then fold over, layer-cake fashion, and press together. Cut in narrow strips, three inches long by an inch wide, and bake fifteen minutes in a hot oven, 400 degrees F.

Swiss Cheese Biscuits

2 cups flour	6 tablespoons Nucoa
4 teaspoons baking powder	2 egg yolks or one egg
1 teaspoon sugar	⅔ cup milk
½ teaspoon salt	½ cup grated Swiss cheese

Sift the dry ingredients together and cut in the Nucoa with the back and edge of a spoon until the consistency of coarse cornmeal. Beat the egg yolks and add the milk; add to the first mixture and mix until blended. Transfer to board dusted with flour and knead for a few seconds. Roll or pat out to one-eighth inch in thickness and sprinkle one-half of the dough with the Swiss cheese. Fold the dough over and shape with a small biscuit cutter. Transfer to a shallow pan or baking sheet rubbed with Nucoa. Brush the tops of the biscuits with a little milk and sprinkle with a little additional cheese. Bake in a very hot oven 400-425 degrees F. for fifteen minutes, or until puffy and brown.

English Tea Biscuits

2 cups flour	6 tablespoons Nucoa
1 tablespoon sugar	½ cup cleaned currants
½ teaspoon salt	½ cup milk
4 teaspoons baking powder	1 egg

Sift the dry ingredients together; with the back and edge of a spoon, cut in the Nucoa until the consistency of coarse cornmeal. Add the currants and moisten the mixture with the beaten egg and the milk combined. Mix until blended. Transfer to a board dusted with flour. Roll or pat to one-half inch in thickness. Shape with a very small biscuit cutter and transfer to a pan rubbed with Nucoa. Arrange the biscuits so they barely touch. Bake in a very hot oven, 400-425 degrees F. for fifteen minutes, or until puffy and brown.

Plain Scones

2 cups flour	2½ teaspoons baking powder
1 tablespoon sugar	½ teaspoon salt
¼ teaspoon baking soda	5 tablespoons Nucoa
¾ cup buttermilk or sour milk	

Sift the dry ingredients together. Cut in the Nucoa until the consistency of coarse cornmeal; add the buttermilk; blend the mixture together; and divide in two portions. Transfer to a board dusted with flour; and roll to a round shape, one-fourth inch in thickness. Cut each round in quarters; and transfer to a baking sheet generously rubbed with Nucoa. Bake in a hot oven, 400 degrees F. for fifteen minutes, or until brown on top. Split; spread with Nucoa, colored golden, and serve hot with marmalade or jam.

Fruit Muffins

¾ cup small moist raisins or mixed raisins, shredded dates and diced figs	4 tablespoons sugar
	¼ teaspoon salt
	1 egg
2 cups wholewheat flour	1¼ cups milk
3 teaspoons baking powder	¼ cup melted Nucoa

Combine the fruits with dry ingredients. Beat the egg in a bowl; add the milk; stir in the dry ingredients; mix thoroughly and then beat in the melted Nucoa. Transfer to small muffin pans lightly rubbed with Nucoa and bake fifteen to twenty minutes in a hot oven, 375 degrees F. Split and serve with Nucoa, colored golden.

Danish Apfelskiver

1½ cups flour	3 eggs
2 teaspoons baking powder	1 cup milk
½ teaspoon salt	3 tablespoons melted Nucoa

Sift the dry ingredients. Beat the egg yolks; and add the milk. Stir into the flour mixture; add the Nucoa and egg whites, whipped stiff. Transfer to hot Apfelskiver pans rubbed with Nucoa or use tiny round muffin pans. Bake about twenty minutes in a hot oven, 375 degrees F.

Sally Lunn

2 eggs	3 teaspoons baking powder
½ cup sugar	½ teaspoon salt
2 cups flour	1 cup milk
	½ cup Nucoa, melted

Beat the eggs and sugar together until creamy. Sift the dry ingredients together; and add alternately with the milk to the first mixture. Beat in the melted Nucoa; and transfer to a shallow loaf cake pan rubbed with Nucoa. Bake in a hot oven, 375 degrees F. for fifteen minutes, or until brown on top.

Rich Gingerbread

½ cup Nucoa	½ teaspoon baking powder
⅓ cup light brown sugar	½ teaspoon salt
1 egg	¾ teaspoon cinnamon
1 cup molasses	1½ teaspoons ginger
2½ cups flour	⅓ teaspoon cloves
1½ teaspoons baking soda	¾ cup hot water

Cream the Nucoa; add the sugar and egg and beat until creamy. Add the molasses and mix until blended. Sift the dry ingredients together; and add to the first mixture. Stir in the hot water; and beat until smooth and free from lumps. Transfer to a shallow loaf-cake pan rubbed with Nucoa; and bake in a moderate oven, 350 degrees F. for forty minutes, or until firm in the center. Cool slightly; break in squares with a fork; and serve while still warm with Nucoa, tinted golden.

Crumb Coffee Cake

2 cups flour	½ cup Nucoa
2 teaspoons baking powder	2 eggs
½ teaspoon salt	⅓ cup milk
1⅓ cups granulated sugar	¾ teaspoon cinnamon
2 tablespoons light brown sugar	

Sift the flour, baking powder and salt together; add the granulated sugar and work in the Nucoa with the finger tips as in making pie crust. Reserve one cup of this mixture. Beat the eggs; add the milk, and stir this into the dry ingredients. Beat until blended and free from lumps. Transfer to a shallow loaf-cake pan rubbed with Nucoa; and sprinkle with the reserved dry mixture combined with the cinnamon and brown sugar. Bake in a very hot oven, 400 degrees F. for twenty-five minutes. Serve cold or hot.

Flanjes

3 cups flour	4 eggs
1 teaspoon baking powder	2¼ cups milk
½ teaspoon salt	5 tablespoons Nucoa, melted
2 tablespoons sugar	½ teaspoon vanilla
Preserved fruit, applesauce, chopped cooked prunes or crushed strawberries or raspberries, sweetened	

Sift the dry ingredients. Beat the egg yolks light. Add the milk; and beat into the first mixture. Stir in the Nucoa and vanilla; add the egg whites, whipped stiff. The mixture should be quite thin. Drop by small tablespoonsful on Nucoa-d pans, leaving enough room for the cakes to spread. Put in a hot oven, 400 degrees F. and bake, turning as soon as they brown on the bottom. Serve spread with the cooked or crushed fruit. If desired the flanjes may be fried in a heavy frying pan with enough Nucoa to barely cover the bottom.

American Griddle Cakes

3 cups flour	2 tablespoons granulated sugar
3 teaspoons baking powder	1 egg
¾ teaspoon salt	2 cups milk
3 tablespoons melted Nucoa	

Sift the dry ingredients together; add the egg, slightly beaten and combined with the milk and melted Nucoa. Beat until the batter is smooth and free from lumps. Heat a pancake griddle or heavy frying pan, and rub with a little Nucoa. Drop the batter on the griddle by large spoonsful. Fry until brown on the bottom and the tops of the cakes are covered with small bubbles. Then turn and bake until brown on the other side. Transfer to a hot plate and serve immediately with plenty of Nucoa, tinted golden, and accompanied by honey, maple syrup, corn syrup, brown sugar syrup or jelly.

Crêpes Suzette

2 eggs	¼ teaspoon salt
1½ cups milk	1 cup cake flour
⅛ teaspoon orange extract	1 tablespoon powdered sugar
⅛ teaspoon lemon extract	Nucoa

Beat the eggs until thick and lemon-colored; add the milk and extracts. Sift the salt, flour and sugar together; and beat in the egg mixture, using a rotary egg beater or wire whip. Heat a heavy frying pan; put in a little Nucoa; and rotate the pan so that the bottom and sides are covered. Drop on the batter by large tablespoonsful. The cakes should be very thin. Cook over a low heat, first on one side; then carefully turn and cook on the other side until a golden brown. Fold over in halves or quarters; transfer to a hot serving plate; pour over Suzette Sauce; and serve.

Suzette Sauce

6 tablespoons granulated sugar	1 cup orange juice
Grated peel ½ orange	1 tablespoon tart jelly or marmalade
Grated peel ¼ lemon	3 tablespoons Nucoa, colored golden

Thoroughly mix the sugar and peel. Add the orange juice; and cook and stir over a moderate heat until the boiling point is reached. Add the jelly or marmalade; simmer five minutes, then add the Nucoa. Cook and stir until well blended and serve. To make this in true French fashion, use three-fourths cup orange juice and add three table-spoons Curaçao and one of brandy to the boiling sauce.

CHEESE DISHES AND OTHER SAVORIES

In the good old days when cooking was cooking, and royalty dined on eighteen courses, an entrée was a dish brought in while the 'removes' (roasts and other important *plats*) were still on the table. The entrée, simple or 'worked,' represented the height of the cook's art, and to give it distinction he seasoned it with a cunning hand and presented it in the fanciest of dishes.

In these more democratic times, the entrée has become the main dish at informal meals, but the adroit cook still gives it her most studious attention, serving it attractively and flavoring it to the best of her ability. Whether the chief ingredient is a savory cheese, or whether palatable left-overs become dainty rechauffés, as the French call warmed-overs, it's the seasoning that does the trick.

Many a successful cook owes her delicious entrées to the use of the New Nucoa. Sweet whole milk blended with the freshest of vegetable oils is responsible for its richness and flavor. Rapid delivery to your grocer by the fastest trucks guarantees its freshness and delicacy.

ALL MEASUREMENTS ARE LEVEL

Cheese Soufflé

4 tablespoons Nucoa	1 cup milk
3 tablespoons flour	1 cup soft bread crumbs
½ teaspoon salt	¾ cup grated American or store cheese
A few grains cayenne	½ teaspoon baking powder
3 eggs	

Melt the Nucoa; add the flour, salt and cayenne; and mix to a smooth paste. Gradually add the milk, and cook and stir until the sauce thickens. Remove from the heat; add the crumbs and cheese, and stir until the latter dissolves. Separate the eggs; beat the yolks until thick and lemon-colored; and add to the cheese mixture. Fold in the baking powder and the egg whites, whipped stiff. Transfer to a baking dish rubbed with Nucoa. Bake in a moderate oven, 350 degrees F. for thirty minutes, or until a knife when inserted in the center comes out clean. Serve immediately.

Italian Gnocchi

2 cups milk	1 cup grated soft American or store
½ cup farina	cheese
1 teaspoon salt	2 eggs
3 tablespoons Nucoa	Grated cheese (additional)

Scald the milk in the top of a double boiler. Gradually add the farina; and cook and stir until the mixture thickens. Add the salt and Nucoa, and continue to cook for twenty minutes, stirring occasionally. Remove from the heat; add the cheese, and stir until the mixture is free from lumps. Separate the eggs; beat the yolks until thick and lemon-colored; and add to the farina mixture. Fold in the egg whites, whipped stiff; and transfer to a shallow loaf-cake pan, rinsed with cold water. Cool, chill, and cut in squares, rounds or in fancy shapes with sandwich cutters. Transfer to a shallow pan rubbed plentifully with Nucoa; sprinkle with the additional cheese; and bake in a hot oven, 375 degrees F. for fifteen minutes, or until brown all over.

English Cheese Pudding

1 quart milk	2 tablespoons Nucoa
2 cups soft bread crumbs	2 cups finely chopped soft American or store cheese
1 teaspoon salt	
¼ teaspoon pepper	¼ teaspoon baking soda
2 eggs	

Scald the milk; add the bread crumbs, salt, pepper and Nucoa; and stir until blended. Add the cheese, baking soda and eggs, well beaten. Transfer to one large or six individual pudding dishes or ramekins rubbed with Nucoa. Place in a pan of hot water; and bake in a moderate oven, 350 degrees F. for forty-five minutes, or until a knife when inserted comes out clean.

Welsh Rabbit

2 tablespoons Nucoa	½ cup beer
½ pound finely chopped American or store cheese	¼ teaspoon salt
	⅛ teaspoon mustard
1 egg	1 teaspoon meat sauce
1 egg yolk	A few grains cayenne

Melt the Nucoa in the top of chafing dish; add the cheese; and cook and stir over a low heat until the cheese melts. Add the egg, egg yolk and beer beaten together; and cook and stir until the mixture thickens. Add the seasonings, stir to blend, and serve immediately on crisp soda crackers, or toast spread with Nucoa, colored golden.

Rich Cheese Sauce

4 tablespoons Nucoa	1½ cups milk
3 tablespoons flour	1 cup finely chopped soft American
½ teaspoon salt	or store cheese (highly flavored)
⅛ teaspoon paprika	

Melt the Nucoa; add the flour and seasonings, and blend. Gradually add the milk; and cook and stir until the sauce thickens. Add the cheese. Place over hot water, or in the top of a double boiler; and cook and stir until the cheese melts.

Broiled Tomatoes with Cheese Sauce

Spread toasted bread with Nucoa; place half a broiled tomato on each slice of toast, and pour over Rich Cheese Sauce. Garnish with parsley and serve.

Quick Spaghetti or Macaroni

Cook until tender one-half pound spaghetti or macaroni in boiling salted water to cover. Drain; combine with Rich Cheese Sauce; and serve plain or place in the oven or under a low broiler heat until brown on top.

Baked Ham and Cheese Rabbit

3 tablespoons Nucoa	1 cup milk
2 tablespoons flour	⅔ cup grated store cheese
¾ teaspoon salt	½ pound cooked drained spaghetti
¼ teaspoon pepper	1½ cups minced cooked ham
¼ cup Nucoa-d bread crumbs	

Melt the Nucoa; add the flour and seasonings, and blend. Gradually add the milk, and cook and stir until the sauce thickens. Remove from the heat; add the cheese, and stir until it melts. In a casserole or baking dish rubbed with Nucoa arrange alternate layers of the spaghetti, ham and cheese sauce mixture. Cover the top with the Nucoa-d bread crumbs; and bake in a hot oven, 375 degrees F. for twenty minutes, or until brown on top.

Note: To prepare Nucoa-d bread crumbs melt two tablespoons Nucoa and stir in three-fourths cup fine dry bread crumbs.

Savory Short Cakes

Follow the recipe for Baking Powder Biscuits. With a biscuit cutter, shape into rounds two inches in diameter and bake as directed. Split; spread with Nucoa and put together and top with any savory shredded or diced meat mixture, put together with a medium thick sauce. Various combinations follow.

Creamed Meat Short Cakes

Prepare shortcake biscuits as directed. Put together and top with creamed chicken, veal, ham or lamb. Garnish with parsley.

Sea Food Short Cakes

Combine one cup cleaned whole shrimps, one-half cup diced cooked lobster and one-half cup flaked crabmeat with one and a half cups medium white sauce and use as a filling for Savory Short Cakes.

Italian Spaghetti

1 pound spaghetti	1 can tomato paste
½ cup Nucoa	Water
3 cloves garlic or ½ cup chopped raw onion	¾ teaspoon salt
	⅛ teaspoon pepper
½ pound chopped raw beef	Parmesan cheese

Boil the spaghetti until tender but not mushy in salted water and drain it. In the meantime put the Nucoa in a small heavy frying pan; add the garlic or onion if used, and sauté until yellow in the Nucoa. Then add the meat and sauté, stirring with a fork until lightly browned. Combine the tomato paste with an equal amount of water; add to the meat mixture and simmer until thick; season with the salt and pepper. Allow thirty minutes to make this sauce. Pour over the spaghetti and pass plenty of Parmesan cheese. American cheese may be substituted.

YEAST BREADS

When cold winds whip up from the Baltic Sea, then the housewives of northern Europe know it's time for hot drinks and crunchy sweet breads. The coffee pot bubbles all day long on the great porcelain stove, and the smell of nut-sprinkled twists, spicy crumb cakes and glazed coffee rings fills the air. Afternoon, morning, evening, whenever friend or neighbor passes by, there is the clink of cups and cheery conversation.

And now modern cooking methods have made it possible for the American homemaker to have all these delicious Old-World yeast breads with minimum labor. Instead of overnight preparation, five hours or less is enough time to prepare any of the recipes given in this book.

When made with the New Nucoa, the flavor of these breads is not only more delicate, but they keep fresh and moist longer than when ordinary shortenings are used. It's the marvelous New Nucoa blend of pasteurized milk and fresh American vegetable oils that does it.

As a spread for fancy breads, hot or cold, nothing quite equals Nucoa. It is always fresh—for it is rushed by truck to the stores as soon as it is made. Be as generous as you like—you can afford to— Nucoa is so inexpensive!

ALL MEASUREMENTS ARE LEVEL

Simple Yeast Rolls

Part I	Part II
1 compressed yeast cake	⅓ cup Nucoa
½ cup water	1 cup tepid water
¼ cup sugar	1 egg
1 cup flour	1½ teaspoons salt
	About 3 cups flour
	Melted Nucoa

Dissolve the yeast cake in the one-half cup tepid water; add the sugar and beat in one cup flour. Cover and set for fifteen minutes in a warm place or until the top is full of bubbles. Next, melt the Nucoa

38

and add it, together with the cup of tepid water and slightly beaten egg, to the sponge. Beat in three cups of the flour mixed with one and one-half teaspoons salt or enough flour to make a dough soft enough to knead. Transfer to a bowl rubbed with Nucoa. Rub over the top of the dough with melted Nucoa. Cover and let stand in a warm place until double in bulk. Cut down with a knife and shape into pocket-book rolls, finger-length rolls, or into cloverleaf rolls. Place in Nucoa-d pans; let stand until double in bulk and bake in a hot oven, 375 degrees F., allowing about thirty minutes. When done, brush the tops with Nucoa. If desired, the dough may be placed in the refrigerator over-night and made up into rolls in the morning.

Nut Bread

1 cup milk	Entire wheat flour to knead, about
1 tablespoon molasses	4 cupsful
1½ tablespoons Nucoa	1½ teaspoons salt
¾ compressed yeast cake	1 cup chopped walnuts, pecans or
3 tablespoons lukewarm water	mixed nuts

Scald the milk and add the molasses and Nucoa; cool until tepid. Dissolve the yeast in the lukewarm water and stir into the first mixture. Then add two cups of flour mixed with the salt and nuts and continue to beat in the flour until the mixture can be kneaded. Knead until it feels elastic when touched with the hand. Put in a bowl rubbed with Nucoa; brush over the top with melted Nucoa. Cover and set aside in a warm place to rise until double in bulk. Then cut down with a knife and shape into two small loaves with as little kneading as possible. Transfer to small bread pans rubbed with Nucoa. Cover and let rise again until double in bulk and bake fifty minutes in a moderately hot oven, 350-375 degrees F. Rub the tops of the loaves when done with Nucoa.

Sweet Swedish Loaf

1 compressed yeast cake	¾ cup melted Nucoa
1 cup tepid water	3 eggs
1½ cups scalded milk	⅔ cup sugar
3 cups flour	1½ tablespoons ground cardamom seeds
1 teaspoon salt	Additional flour

Dissolve the yeast in the water; add to the milk; beat in the three cups of flour with the salt. Cover; and let rise until spongy. Then add the Nucoa and the eggs and sugar, beaten together. Add half the cardamom seeds, and flour to knead. Transfer to long, narrow, Nucoa-d pans; cover and let rise until doubled. Bake in a moderately hot oven, 350-375 degrees F. about forty-five minutes. When almost done brush over with a cornstarch glaze, granulated sugar and the remaining cardamom seeds. To make the glaze, add two tablespoons cornstarch to one cup cold water; and stir until it looks clear.

Coffee Ring

Follow the recipe for Sweet Swedish Loaf, substituting for the cardamom seeds, one-half cup mixed chopped raisins, citron and nuts. After kneading, form the dough into long strips and transfer to a Nucoa-d cooky sheet. Shape to form a circle; slash at intervals to form petals. Let rise until doubled. Bake as directed, using instead of cardamom seeds on the top, chopped nut meats; or use the creamy icing given in this book.

Scotch Oatmeal Muffins

2 cups scalded milk	4 tablespoons Nucoa
⅓ cup granulated or brown sugar	1 compressed yeast cake
1 teaspoon salt	½ cup lukewarm water
1 cup rolled oats	2 cups all-purpose flour
2 cups entire wheat flour	

Pour the scalded milk into a bowl; add the sugar, salt, oatmeal and Nucoa, and let stand until tepid. Then dissolve the yeast in the lukewarm water; add to the first mixture and beat in the two flours. Cover and set in a warm place to rise. When double in bulk beat again with a spoon. Rub muffin pans with the Nucoa and half-fill with the oatmeal mixture. Cover and let rise again until light. Bake about thirty minutes in a moderately hot oven, 350-375 degrees F. Rub the tops of the muffins with Nucoa when done.

Viennese Christmas Coffee Cake

2 cups scalded milk	1 teaspoon salt
1½ compressed yeast cakes	½ cup Nucoa
¼ cup tepid water	½ cup sugar
About 5 cups all-purpose flour	Juice and grated rind 1 lemon
2 beaten eggs	Sugar, cinnamon, blanched almonds, and candied cherries

Scald the milk; when cooled add the yeast dissolved in the tepid water, and beat in two cups flour to make a batter. Cover and let rise until light and spongy; then add the other ingredients in the order given, and flour to make a dough that can be handled. Reserve sugar, cinnamon, almonds and cherries for decorating. Knead until elastic, then set aside until light. Cut down and put into Nucoa-d pans in sheets an inch and a half thick. Let rise until double in bulk; brush over with melted Nucoa and sprinkle with sugar and cinnamon mixed together. Bake one-half hour in a moderately hot oven, 350-375 degrees F. When partially baked decorate with some whole blanched almonds and shredded candied cherries.

SANDWICHES

Invented by the sporting English Earl of Sandwich who couldn't take time from hunting for lunch, the sandwich has traveled around the world and varies with latitude and longitude.

Italy splits a bread roll, claps it over garlic-laden sausage and makes a meal on it; Scandinavia and Austria serve tidbits on dark bread as appetizers; but it is America that has given the sandwich its amazing versatility.

Whether the occasion calls for a hearty picnic or luncheon sandwich, toasted or layered like a modern skyscraper, or a dainty teatime sandwich, or a tempting appetizer, there are two essentials—bread that is soft and fresh, and a delicious spread that will not break and crumble the bread.

The consistency of the New Nucoa makes it the perfect sandwich spread. Use it plain, simply colored golden with the wafer from the package, or mix it with minced ham, pickle or other savory bits from the refrigerator and keep as an emergency spread.

ALL MEASUREMENTS ARE LEVEL

Scandinavian Open Sandwiches

1. Spread the bread or toast with colored Nucoa; cover with thin slices of cooked pork. Decorate with pickled beets and 'cracklings'; and sprinkle with chives, if desired.

2. Spread the bread or toast with Nucoa, colored golden; put on this a piece, cut to fit, of thin fried fish. Garnish with slices of cucumber and lettuce. Pass tomato sauce, if desired.

3. Spread the bread or toast with Nucoa, colored golden; cover with boiled or fried shrimps; and spread with a little sauce tartare—(if hot, use Hollandaise Sauce). Garnish with parsley or cress.

4. Spread the bread or toast with Nucoa, colored golden; sprinkle

with shredded anchovies in oil; cover with a thin slice of roast beef; spread this with prepared horseradish; garnish with pickles.

5. Spread the bread or toast wth Nucoa, colored golden; cover with tart jelly; place three small chicken patties in the center of each. Garnish with sweet pickles.

Note: If toast is used, the meat or fish covering should be hot. With bread it may be cold.

Delmonico Sandwiches

5 tablespoons Nucoa	2½ cups finely minced chicken,
6 tablespoons flour	ham, lamb, veal, tongue or
¼ teaspoon salt	corned beef
⅛ teaspoon pepper	Mustard or meat sauce (optional)
1 cup top cream	Bread

Barely melt the Nucoa in a double boiler top. Remove from the heat and stir in the flour and seasonings, preferably using a wire whisk. Then return to the heat and add the cream a little at a time, stirring all the while. When very thick and creamy, cook over hot water for five minutes; then add the meat; a dash of mustard or meat sauce may be stirred in. Cool and use as a spreading for sandwiches made with two slices of thinly cut bread of any kind.

Three-Layer Sandwiches

½ pound cream cheese	2 small minced sweet green peppers
¼ cup pickle relish	½ cup minced nut meats
1 cup minced ham	Nucoa, colored golden
⅓ cup grated carrot	White and entire wheat bread

These sandwiches are put together in layer-cake style, each layer consisting of a different filling. These fillings are made as follows: For the first; cream together one-third cup Nucoa, the cream cheese and pickle relish. For the second; cream together the minced ham, carrot and one-third cup Nucoa. For the third; cream together the green peppers, chopped nuts and one-third cup Nucoa. Put together with the white and entire wheat bread alternating. The crusts should be removed. The filled bread should then be wrapped in a damp napkin and placed in the refrigerator for a few hours. To serve, slice down like a layer cake.

Grilled Sandwiches

Slice white or entire wheat bread a scant fourth-inch thick. Put together with the desired filling, spread on both sides with Nucoa. Place in a Nucoa-d pan, put under the broiler and grill until golden brown, first on one side, then the other. If made thin, the filling will be heated through. Suitable fillings are:

1. Thin slices of cheese sprinkled with mustard.

2. Thin slices of ham, cold beef steak, roast beef or lamb. (Spread the meat with Nucoa, blended with a little horseradish mustard.)

3. A thin spreading of minced salmon, crabmeat or tuna fish mixed with a little mayonnaise.

4. Thin chopped beef patties, broiled rare.

VEGETABLES

And what shall we have for the vegetable course? It's a question never omitted by the French chef. Vegetables, in his eyes, are too important to be relegated to second place. He serves them as a separate course, cooked to perfection, seasoned with understanding.

He takes infinite pains to conserve their natural flavors and to heighten them. How does he do it? First by baking or steaming the vegetable, or by cooking it in a minimum of water, which all but evaporates by the time the vegetable is done. He uses a soupçon— just a suspicion—of sugar, and sufficient salt. And he always uses some ingredient which will supply richness and intensify the delicate individual flavor of whatever vegetable he is preparing.

French chefs, as well as homemakers in America, find that the New Nucoa meets these requirements. It is a blend of sweet whole milk and fresh American vegetable oils, both of them rich in nutritive value. Because it is suitable for table use it is good enough for the seasoning of the most delicate vegetable. Even the commonest vegetables may be made delicious by seasoning with plenty of Nucoa—and you can afford to use it, too, for Nucoa costs about half as much as other fine seasonings for vegetables.

Plain-Cooked Vegetables

Several principles must be followed in the plain cooking of vegetables in order to retain full food value and flavor. To do this:

1. Steam or bake without peeling whenever possible. Allow one-fourth longer cooking time than when boiled. Rub the skins of vegetables to be baked with New Nucoa to keep them soft and to add flavor.
2. If to be boiled, cook the vegetables in water barely to cover, containing a half teaspoon each of salt and sugar. To hasten the cookery, large vegetables may be diced or sliced, and beans may be shredded, or cut in Juliennes. Use the resulting liquid as a sauce with the vegetables or in making soup.

3. Season plain-cooked vegetables with a little pepper, and with a tablespoonful of the New Nucoa, tinted golden, for each pint of vegetable. This adds nutriment and deliciousness and brings the flavor of the vegetable up and out.

4. Aim to bring out or star the flavor of each vegetable.

In planning vegetable or 'garden meals,' do not use more than three or four vegetables cooked by one or more methods; and balance each menu with cheese, eggs, nuts or milk, for most vegetables contain very little protein, the food element that builds muscle.

ALL MEASUREMENTS ARE LEVEL

Whipped Potatoes

6 large potatoes	1 teaspoon salt
2 tablespoons Nucoa	⅛ teaspoon pepper
¼ cup heated milk	

Peel and steam or boil the potatoes until tender; then shake over the heat until dried out. Put the potatoes through a potato ricer. Add the remaining ingredients and whip with a wire whisk until creamy.

Potato Crust for Meat Pies

Add a beaten egg yolk to Whipped Potatoes and pile lightly on a hot meat or fish pie; brown in a hot oven.

Flaky Boiled Potatoes

Peel twelve medium-sized potatoes and cook until tender in boiling water to cover allowing one-half teaspoon each of salt and sugar; then drain. Shake over a low heat until the potatoes look flaky; then measure into the kettle two tablespoons of Nucoa, and when it melts, roll the potatoes in it until it has been absorbed.

Parslied Potatoes

Sprinkle flaky boiled potatoes just before serving with a little finely minced parsley. Keep the heat low.

Cottage Fried Potatoes

6 medium-sized boiled potatoes	⅛ teaspoon pepper
½ teaspoon salt	4 tablespoons Nucoa

Cut the potatoes in small thin pieces; melt the Nucoa in a medium-sized frying pan; add the potatoes and seasonings and fry until golden brown, turning occasionally. Keep the heat low.

Quick Potatoes O'Brien

3 cups diced cooked potatoes	1 medium-sized onion, diced
1 large green pepper, diced	Nucoa
1 small sweet red pepper, diced	Salt and pepper

Into a heavy frying pan put two generous tablespoons of Nucoa and sauté the potatoes in this until brown, stirring occasionally. In the meantime, melt two level tablespoonsful of Nucoa in a small frying pan and in this sauté the peppers and onion, taking care not to burn them. Keep the heat low. Dust the frying potatoes with salt and pepper. When done, transfer to a serving dish and pour the pepper and onion mixture over the potatoes.

Russian Potato Pancakes

6 medium-sized potatoes	¾ teaspoon salt
2 eggs	⅛ teaspoon pepper
2 tablespoons flour	Nucoa

Wash, peel and grate the potatoes. Drain off the water that accumulates. Separate the eggs; beat the whites stiff and the yolks until lemon-colored. Add the yolks, flour, salt and pepper to the potatoes. Then fold in the whites, stiffly whipped. Melt enough Nucoa in a heavy frying pan to barely cover the bottom. When bubbling hard, drop in the potato mixture by tablespoonsful and fry slowly, first on one side, then the other until browned. If necessary, add a little more Nucoa from time to time.

Potatoes Au Gratin

1 quart chopped peeled raw potatoes	1¼ teaspoons salt
1 cup grated well-flavored store cheese	¼ teaspoon pepper
	1½ cups milk
2½ tablespoons flour	3 tablespoons Nucoa

Rub a baking dish with Nucoa; combine the potatoes, cheese, flour and seasonings, mixing well. Transfer to a baking dish; pour the milk in; enough should be used so that it is barely visible through the top layer of potatoes. Dot with the Nucoa. Cover and bake thirty minutes in a moderately hot oven, 350-375 degrees F. Then uncover to brown, allowing about fifteen minutes longer.

Fried Tomatoes

6 medium-sized firm tomatoes	1 egg
¼ cup flour	¾ cup fine dry breadcrumbs
1 teaspoon sugar	Water
½ teaspoon salt	Nucoa

Wash the tomatoes and cut out the stem ends; cut the tomatoes crosswise in half-inch slices. Dip in the flour which should be mixed with the sugar and salt. Beat the egg; combine it with two tablespoons of water and dip the tomato slices in it. Cover them with crumbs and then sauté slowly until golden, first on one side then the other in enough Nucoa to barely cover the bottom of a heavy frying pan.

Italian Style String Beans

1 quart shredded string or wax beans	3 minced mint leaves (optional)
	½ teaspoon salt
1 cup canned tomatoes	2 tablespoons Nucoa
1 clove garlic, minced or 2 tablespoons minced onion	

Steam or boil and drain the string beans as usual. Add the tomato, the garlic or onion, salt, mint leaves and Nucoa and simmer twenty minutes.

Italian Eggplant

1 medium-sized eggplant	Salt and pepper
Flour	2 tablespoons minced parsley
2 eggs	Nucoa
¼ cup grated Parmesan or American cheese	2 cups canned tomatoes

Slice the eggplant a quarter of an inch thick. It is not necessary to peel it or to squeeze out the juice. Dip each slice in flour. Slightly beat the eggs and add the cheese, one-fourth teaspoon black pepper, one-half teaspoon salt, and the parsley. Dip the floured slices in this mixture and fry first on one side then on the other until browned in Nucoa, just enough to barely cover the bottom of a heavy frying pan. Remove the eggplant. There should be two tablespoons of Nucoa left in the pan. Add the tomato and simmer ten minutes. Then place the eggplant in layers in Nucoa-d baking dish and pour over the tomato mixture. Bake twenty minutes in a moderate oven, 350 degrees F.

Broccoli, Artichoke or Asparagus Hollandaise

Prepare broccoli, globe artichokes or asparagus according to the usual recipe. Drain and serve very hot with Hollandaise Sauce. (See section on Savory Sauces.)

Sautéd Mushrooms

1 pound mushrooms	Few grains nutmeg
½ teaspoon salt	4 tablespoons Nucoa

Pick over the mushrooms and wash them. Slice lengthwise through cap and stem. Melt the Nucoa in a medium-sized frying pan and add the mushrooms and seasonings. Cover and sauté slowly twelve to fifteen minutes.

Peas au Jus

3 cups fresh young peas	½ teaspoon sugar
1 small onion, chopped	⅛ teaspoon pepper
½ teaspoon salt	3 tablespoons Nucoa

Put all the ingredients together in a heavy rather deep kettle. Sprinkle the peas with water. Cover very tightly and cook over a slow heat until the peas are tender, about thirty minutes.

Sautéd Corn

2½ tablespoons Nucoa	½ teaspoon salt
3 cups kernels, cut from raw green corn	⅛ teaspoon pepper
½ teaspoon sugar	

Melt the Nucoa in a heavy frying pan. When bubbling hard, stir in the corn and seasonings and slowly sauté for five minutes.

Savory Onion Pie

2 large slices bacon, diced	1 tablespoon Nucoa
2 cups diced onion	1 tablespoon flour
1 teaspoon salt	1 egg
1 teaspoon sugar	¾ cup milk
⅛ teaspoon pepper	Rich Short Pie Crust
	(See section on Pies)

Cook the bacon until crisp; add the onions, seasonings and Nucoa. Steam ten minutes. Combine the flour and the egg, beaten. Add the milk; stir in the onion mixture. Pour into a pie plate, lined with the pastry. Bake in a hot oven for the first ten minutes, 375 degrees F., then moderate it and bake for twenty minutes longer.

Portuguese Potato and Meat Left-Overs

Cold roast meat, any kind	Salt and pepper
Cold boiled potatoes	Nucoa

Slice the meat in even finger-length strips and slice the potatoes lengthwise. Melt enough Nucoa in a heavy frying pan to barely cover the bottom. When bubbling hard, put in the meat and potato and brown first on one side, then the other. Dust with salt and pepper and serve very hot.

SEA FOOD

The first explorers of the world were fishermen. Venturing far out to sea, their little boats were blown out of their course, and quite unexpectedly these honest providers found themselves breakfasting on a foreign strand. Even the coast of America probably figured in fishermen's gossip long before kings and queens got interested in it as a commercial enterprise.

For fish has been, and still is, one of the favorite foods of the earth. It's one of the most delicious too, when properly cooked. The pickled fish of Scandinavia, or the richly spiced bouillabaise of the Mediterranean, do not always tempt our American palates, but there's many an interesting hint for appetizing dishes in this foreign cookery.

Fish, if it is to be as delicious as it deserves to be, must be cooked properly. Slow cooking at a low temperature—never more than 350 degrees F.—is all important. And since fish contains little or no fat, this deficiency must be overcome in the preparation. Whether fish is fried, broiled, sautéd, baked or served with a sauce, the New Nucoa forms a perfect nutritive balance. But more important still—the fish becomes more tender, more appetizing, more digestible when Nucoa is used.

Everyone who has vacationed near the sea shore has participated in a clam bake—the great hole lined with rocks, the blazing fire raked away, then lobsters, corn, clams, all covered with seaweed and left to bake. But did you ever try a fish bake in a closely covered pot in your oven?

Or have you initiated your family into that most American of meals, a sea-food dinner? Here is a menu that will please them. Steamed little neck clams, served with a sauce of melted Nucoa, tinted golden, and mixed with catsup; Maine fish or lobster chowder; stuffed baked fish; sliced tomatoes or a green salad; and a fruit dessert.

To Broil Fish

Whole Fish—Remove the head of the fish; split down the back so it will lay flat, and remove the bones if there is time. Rub the broiler, or if the meshes are too coarse, a pan, thickly with Nucoa and place the fish on it. Dust with salt and pepper, dot with Nucoa and place near the heat to sear it quickly. Then cook more gently, turning once. Allow twenty minutes for a fish weighing a pound and a half. After broiling, spread with a little Nucoa, colored golden, and reheat a moment, or serve with Maître d'Hôtel Sauce. As fish is deficient in fat the use of Nucoa tends to make it juicy and tender.

Fish Fillets—Follow the procedure outlined above, allowing eight minutes for the broiling of thin fillets like flounder, and from twelve to fifteen minutes for halibut, salmon, cod, haddock or other thick fish fillets.

To Bone a Fish—Begin at the tail end; slip the knife, which should be thin and sharp, between the flesh and the bones, working up the backbone. Do this on both sides.

Halibut Grill or Seafood Platter

Broil halibut steaks. Arrange on a platter and serve garnished with Simplified French Fried Shrimps, scallops and oysters.

Pan-Fried Fish

This recipe may be used in preparing trout, smelt, butterfish, small flounders or any other small fish.

Remove the heads, fins and tails. Clean and wash the fish and drain on paper towels. Season with salt and pepper and dust lightly with flour. Melt enough Nucoa in a heavy frying pan to cover the bottom to a depth of one-eighth inch. When bubbling hard, put in the fish and fry slowly and steadily until golden. Keep the heat low. Turn with a pancake turner. If necessary, add a little more Nucoa putting it in from the side of the pan and tipping the pan so that it will run over the bottom. Allow about ten minutes for the fish cookery. Transfer to a heated platter and serve garnished with lemon slices, baked tomato slices, sautéd corn, cole slaw or bouquets of cress.

Fillets of Codfish Holland Style

1½ pounds fillets of codfish	3 tablespoons Nucoa
1 pint French potato balls (or diced raw potato)	½ cup chopped chives or onion
	¼ cup water
1 teaspoon salt	2 tablespoons lemon juice
⅛ teaspoon pepper	Hollandaise Sauce

Rub a baking pan or large fire-proof platter with Nucoa. Place the fillets upon this. Surround with the potato. Dust with salt and pepper; dot with Nucoa and sprinkle with the chives. Pour in the water and lemon juice. Bake forty-five minutes in a moderate oven, 350-375 degrees F. Serve with Hollandaise Sauce.

Fish 'n Chips

For six people select two pounds of haddock, cod or flounder fillets. Dust with salt and pepper. Roll in flour, then in a slightly-beaten egg mixed with two tablespoons milk, and coat with fine dry bread crumbs. Set aside until time to fry. In the meantime, prepare the potato 'chips' as follows: Peel and with a lattice cutter slice the potatoes to one-eighth inch in thickness. Let stand in cold water ten minutes to crisp. Then drain on a towel. Put enough Nucoa in a heavy warmed frying pan to make a depth of one-half inch, when melted. When the Nucoa is bubbling hard, put in the potatoes and fry slowly until golden. This takes about seven minutes. Drain on crumpled paper and place in the oven to keep warm. Into the same Nucoa put the prepared fish, frying it until golden, first on one side then the other, using a steady low heat. It will take about twelve minutes. Drain on crumpled paper and serve with the 'chips' in a big dish.

Note: Any remaining Nucoa may be strained through a fine sieve and used for later frying, because Nucoa does not take up fish flavor.

Baltimore Crab Cakes

3 cups crab meat	Few grains pepper
1 small egg	⅛ teaspoon paprika
½ tablespoon flour	½ teaspoon lemon juice
½ teaspoon salt	Nucoa

Mix together the crab, egg, flour, seasonings and lemon juice. Shape into cakes, allowing a tablespoonful each. Roll them in flour. In the meantime, melt enough Nucoa in a heavy, warmed frying pan to cover the bottom to the depth of one-eighth inch. When bubbling hard put in the crab cakes and brown slightly, first on one side, then the other until golden. Keep the heat low. Serve plain or with a Rich White Sauce. Garnish with parsley and lemon slices.

Lobster Cakes

Follow the recipe for Baltimore Crab Cakes substituting fresh or canned lobster.

Salmon or Tuna Fish Cakes

Follow the recipe for Baltimore Crab Cakes substituting canned tuna fish or salmon.

Minced Salmon Pie

½ pound canned salmon	½ teaspoon salt
½ cup soft bread crumbs	⅛ teaspoon pepper
¼ cup milk	⅛ teaspoon nutmeg
2 eggs	½ tablespoon minced parsley
½ tablespoon lemon juice	(optional)
3 tablespoons melted Nucoa	Short Biscuit Meat Pie Pastry
	(See Meat Section)

Line an earthenware or glass pie plate with the pastry. Remove the skin and bones from the salmon; mince the salmon fine and combine with the bread crumbs scalded in the milk, the egg yolks, lightly beaten, the lemon juice, the Nucoa, seasonings and parsley. Fold in the egg whites; spread in the crust-lined plate and bake in a very hot oven, 375-400 degrees F. for ten minutes. Then reduce the heat slightly and continue to bake until the crust is brown and the center is firm to the touch. Allow about thirty minutes. Serve garnished with parsley, sliced lemon or broiled tomatoes.

Simplified French Fried Shrimps

2 pounds fresh shrimps	Salt and pepper
Flour	Nucoa

Remove the shells from the shrimps and cut out the dark line along the back which is the intestinal vein. Dip the shrimps in flour mixed with a little salt and pepper. In the meantime, warm a heavy frying pan and into it put enough Nucoa to make a depth of one-half inch. When melted, heat until bubbling; put in the shrimps and fry slowly until golden brown, turning when brown on one side to cook the

other. Drain on crumpled paper and serve with Maître d'Hôtel Sauce
or catsup.

Note: Pour any remaining Nucoa through a fine sieve and use for
future Simplified French Frying.

Simplified French Fried Scallops or Oysters

1½ pints medium-sized scallops or oysters	2 tablespoons milk
	1 egg
Salt and pepper	Fine dry bread crumbs
Flour	Nucoa

Dust the scallops with salt and pepper. Then roll them in flour. Beat
the egg slightly with two tablespoons milk and coat the scallops with
this. Roll them in the crumbs. In the meantime, heat the Nucoa as
described in the previous recipe for French Fried Shrimps and fry the
scallops as directed.

SAVORY SAUCES

English and French cooks, so it is said, carry on a spirited and wordy warfare across the Channel. The subject of their encounters—Sauces. Say the French, the English have but one sauce. John Bull retorts that Monsieur le Chef masks everything, even boiled potatoes, in one of his innumerable sauces.

But as non-combatants, we must admit that the right sauce compounded in the right way can make a cook's name and fame. But there's the rub—the ingredients must be the best, and they must be combined with a skillful hand.

The New Nucoa lends that richness and flavor—with economy—that is so necessary to the success of savory sauces. It is made from sweet pasteurized milk blended with the finest American vegetable oils—these, the master cook knows, have been ingredients of the most delicious sauces for hundreds of years.

ALL MEASUREMENTS ARE LEVEL

Maître d'Hôtel Sauce
(To be served with steak or broiled fish)

⅓ cup Nucoa, colored golden	Few grains cayenne
1 tablespoon minced parsley	1 tablespoon lemon juice
¼ teaspoon salt	Few drops onion juice

Measure the Nucoa into a small bowl and gradually cream in the remaining ingredients. Place on ice to chill; then shape into small patties or balls and put one on each serving of meat or fish just before it is passed.

Hollandaise Sauce

½ cup Nucoa, colored golden	1½ tablespoons lemon juice
1 teaspoon flour	⅛ teaspoon paprika
4 egg yolks	⅛ teaspoon salt
½ cup boiling water	

Cream together the Nucoa and flour; gradually work in the egg yolks one at a time; then cream in the lemon juice, salt and paprika; add the boiling water. Cook and stir over hot water until the sauce is thick and smooth.

Indian Sauce

1½ tablespoons Nucoa	Grated rind ¼ lemon
1½ tablespoons flour	½ cup chopped tomato
1 cup soup stock	A bit of bay leaf
1 teaspoon curry powder	Few grains salt
½ tablespoon minced onion	Few grains cayenne

Melt the Nucoa. Add the flour and gradually the soup stock. Stir in the curry powder, mixed with a teaspoonful of cold water. Add the remaining ingredients to the sauce and season to taste. Simmer about ten minutes.

Brown Mushroom Sauce
(Use with vegetable plates, steak, boiled beef, meat croquettes, etc.)

4 tablespoons Nucoa	¼ teaspoon kitchen bouquet or
¾ cup shredded mushrooms	meat sauce (optional)
4 tablespoons flour	2 cups brown soup stock
1 teaspoon scraped onion	Salt and pepper

Melt the Nucoa; add the mushrooms and sauté slowly for five minutes. Stir in the flour and cook until it turns golden, stirring occasionally. Add the scraped onion, the kitchen bouquet or meat sauce if used, and gradually stir in the soup stock. Cook and stir until boiling point has been reached. Add salt and pepper to taste.

Spanish Sauce
(Use with poached or scrambled eggs, plain omelette, fish or meat balls)

2 tablespoons Nucoa	⅛ teaspoon pepper
1 tablespoon chopped green pepper	1½ cups stewed and strained
1 tablespoon chopped onion	tomatoes
1½ tablespoons flour	1 teaspoon capers (optional)
1 teaspoon salt	4 sliced olives (optional)
½ cup shredded mushrooms (optional)	

Melt the Nucoa; add the green pepper and onion and sauté until light yellow. Then stir in the flour and seasonings and gradually add the tomato. Cook and stir until boiling point is reached. Then add the capers, olives or mushrooms if used (one or all of them may be added), and simmer five minutes longer.

Thin White Cream Sauce
(For use with vegetables)

1½ tablespoons Nucoa	⅓ teaspoon salt
1½ tablespoons flour	Few grains pepper
1½ cups milk	

Medium Thick White Cream Sauce
(For use with meats, fish, eggs and in making escalloped dishes)

3 tablespoons Nucoa   ⅓ teaspoon salt
3 tablespoons flour   Few grains pepper
1½ cups milk

Thick White Cream Sauce
(For use in making meat and fish loaves, binding together the ingredients for croquettes, etc.)

4 tablespoons Nucoa   ¼ teaspoon salt
½ cup flour   ⅛ teaspoon pepper
1 cup milk

The preceding three sauces are all made in the same way:

Melt the Nucoa in a small saucepan; remove from the heat and stir in the flour and seasonings, preferably with a wire whisk. Return to the heat and add the milk a little at a time, mixing continually and being sure that the sauce thickens with each addition of milk before more is added. Bring to a rapid boil.

À la King Sauce
(Used in preparing chicken, tuna fish, ham or eggs à la king)

Follow the recipe for Medium Thick White Cream Sauce with this exception: Add to the melted Nucoa one-half a green pepper cut in squares, one-half a pimiento cut in squares and one-half cup shredded mushrooms and sauté slowly three minutes before adding the flour.

Béchamel Sauce
(Use with chicken, eggs, mushrooms, oysters, and escalloped savory meat dishes)

Follow the recipe for Medium Thick White Cream Sauce substituting three-quarters of a cup chicken stock for three-quarters of a cup of the milk. To turn into yellow Béchamel Sauce, stir in just before serving two egg yolks, diluted with two tablespoons of top milk.

MEATS

Stroll leisurely through the cobbled village streets of France, Italy or Spain. Through half-opened cottage doors come whiffs of spicy tantalizing odors. Within, bubble lazily, over charcoal fires, in huge pots and casseroles, rich savory stews and ragoûts.

In these thickly populated foreign lands there are no Great Plains, as in our own country, to supply tender juicy cuts of meat. Meats, oftentimes imported from distant South America or Australia, are expensive and scarce.

But foreign home makers, undaunted, have mixed wits with cookery, and out of their iron kettles, have come a host of appetizing dishes, all based on the most inexpensive cuts. These native miracles are performed by slow cooking, by using the tasty herbs and spices of home fields, and by basting with olive oil, butter or cream or whatever such ingredient is plentiful in their country and therefore economical.

In planning this chapter, we searched far and wide for delicious economical meat dishes, as prepared by the women of many lands. We have gathered recipes sufficient for two whole weeks of dinners. Let them add flavor and variety to your meals. They will prove real money savers, too.

Season them imaginatively, cook them over slow fires, and baste them frequently with the New Nucoa, the rich double-purpose food that is truly American. For it is made of whole pasteurized milk and fresh American vegetable oils blended together. Let the richness of the New Nucoa seep into the meat and tender-ize it. Nucoa is so inexpensive that you can use it generously. And if in an extravagant moment, you broil a porterhouse or bake a plump fillet of beef, baste that too with Nucoa. You will marvel at the resulting delicacy of flavor.

ALL MEASUREMENTS ARE LEVEL

Medallions of Veal

4 tablespoons Nucoa	1 teaspoon salt
1 clove garlic, peeled, or ½ slice onion	⅛ teaspoon pepper
	Spanish Sauce
1½ pounds veal steak, sliced very thin	

Melt the Nucoa. Slightly brown the garlic (or onion) in it and re-move. Brown the veal in the Nucoa, first on one side then the other, allowing about eight minutes and using a moderate heat. Dust while cooking with the salt and pepper. Serve at once with the sauce poured over.

Short Biscuit Meat Pie Pastry

3 cups flour	¾ teaspoon salt
5 teaspoons baking powder	½ cup Nucoa
1 cup water	

Sift the dry ingredients together. Measure in three tablespoons of Nucoa and chop it into the flour with the back and edge of a spoon. When the Nucoa is in the form of large flakes, add the water, mixing it in quickly. Transfer the dough to a slightly floured board and roll to one-half inch in thickness. Spread it with two tablespoons of the Nucoa to within one-half inch of the edge. Then fold it over and press the edges together. Roll it again; spread with two more table-spoons of the remaining Nucoa and roll it as previously directed. Then spread with the balance of the Nucoa; roll again; and use as desired.

English Beefsteak Pie

2 pounds bottom round or flank steak	½ teaspoon thyme
1½ teaspoons salt	½ bay leaf
⅛ teaspoon pepper	1 tablespoon parsley
¼ cup flour	1¼ cups boiling water
1 parboiled lamb's kidney	Nucoa
¼ cup minced onion	Short Biscuit Meat Pie Pastry

First parboil the kidney by cooking it fifteen minutes in salted boiling water to cover. Then dice the kidney; cut the steak in thin strips. Combine the flour, salt and pepper and roll the two meats in this. Then arrange them in alternating layers in a Nucoa-d baking dish, sprinkling with the onion, thyme, crushed bay leaf and parsley. Pour over this the boiling water. There should be enough to moisten it. Dot with the Nucoa. Cover with a crust made from the Short Biscuit Meat Pie Pastry. Slash this to allow the steam to escape and bake two hours in a very slow oven not more than 325 degrees F.

Mutton Chops, Swedish Style

2 tablespoons melted Nucoa	½ teaspoon crushed pickle spice
½ tablespoon vinegar	6 lamb or mutton shoulder chops
1 teaspoon salt	Bread crumbs
1 pint Norwegian savory apple sauce	

Combine the Nucoa, vinegar, salt and spices. Rub this into the chops, cover, and let stand two hours. Roll in the crumbs and broil eight minutes. Serve with the sauce. To make this, stir a tablespoon of Nucoa and one of horseradish into a pint of hot sweetened apple sauce.

Stuffed Mexican Steak

1½ pounds flank steak	3 tablespoons Nucoa
Chili Stuffing	Salt and pepper

Order the steak dressed, with the fat removed and the meat scored on both sides. Spread the stuffing on the steak to within an inch of the edge. Roll up as in making jelly roll, and tie securely. Dust with salt and pepper. Place in a heavy kettle or roasting pan, and brown all over in the Nucoa. Add just enough water to keep the meat from sticking. Cover closely, and simmer an hour and a half like a pot roast, or until nearly tender. Replenish the water if necessary. Uncover and roast until well browned, about thirty minutes longer. Potatoes, onion, or whole tomatoes may be cooked with the meat, if desired.

Chili Stuffing

2 cups soft bread crumbs	1 tablespoon chili powder
2 tablespoons melted Nucoa	2 chopped green peppers
¾ teaspoon salt	1 good-sized onion, chopped
¼ teaspoon pepper	1 cup canned tomatoes, well drained

Combine the ingredients in the order given and use as directed.

Veal and Ham Pie

1½ pounds veal from the knuckle	1 good-sized onion, sliced
3 tablespoons flour	1½ cups diced potato
2 tablespoons Nucoa	½ pound sliced smoked ham
2 cups soup stock	Short Biscuit Meat Pie Pastry

Cut the veal in small pieces. Roll in the flour and sauté slowly until well browned in the Nucoa. Add the soup stock and onion and bring to boiling point. Arrange in a Nucoa-d baking dish in alternate layers with the potato and the ham cut in short narrow strips. Cover closely and bake in a moderate oven, 350 degrees F. for an hour and a half or until the veal is tender. Cover with a crust made from the Short Biscuit Meat Pie Pastry. Slash this to allow the steam to escape and bake twenty minutes in a slightly hotter oven, 375 degrees F.

French Veal Casserole

1 teaspoon sugar	A little grated lemon rind
3 tablespoons Nucoa	1 teaspoon salt
¼ cup finely minced onion	¼ teaspoon pepper
4 pounds knuckle of veal, diced	1 quart boiling water
3 tablespoons flour	1 cup top cream or undiluted evaporated milk

Measure the sugar into a frying pan and place over a low heat. When brown, add the Nucoa and when melted the onion. Stir until yellowed. Then add the veal and cook until lightly browned, about twenty minutes. Next, stir in the flour, add the lemon rind and seasonings and when thoroughly blended, the boiling water. Cover closely and simmer or bake until the veal is tender, about two hours. Pour in the cream or evaporated milk; bring to boiling point and serve with whipped potato or with boiled or curried rice.

Indian Meat Cake Platter

3 cups minced cold beef	½ teaspoon salt
1 medium-sized onion, minced	⅛ teaspoon pepper
1 clove garlic, minced	⅛ teaspoon nutmeg
2 teaspoons parsley	¼ cup milk
1 tomato, chopped	Flour
1 small sweet pepper, minced	Nucoa for frying
1 egg	Boiled rice
2 teaspoons curry powder	Indian sauce

Combine the meat, onion, garlic, parsley, tomato, sweet pepper, egg, seasonings and milk. Mix very thoroughly. Divide by tablespoonsful into small flat cakes. Dust these with flour; and brown in Nucoa. Then cook slowly, about ten minutes. Make a mound of boiled rice on a good-sized platter. Arrange the meat cakes around this; and pour the Indian Sauce over the rice. (See section on Savory Sauces.)

Vienna Loaf

1 cup milk	1 tablespoon scraped onion
½ cup soft bread crumbs	½ teaspoon poultry seasoning
3 cups cold cooked meat, ground	½ teaspoon salt
1 egg	⅛ teaspoon pepper

Short Biscuit Meat Pie Pastry

Scald the milk, add the crumbs and stir to make a paste. Add to the meat; stir in the egg unbeaten; add the onion and seasonings and mix thoroughly; form into a loaf. Cover this with Short Biscuit Meat Pie Pastry, rolled to one-eighth inch in thickness. Place in a Nucoa-d pan and bake forty minutes in a moderately hot oven, 350 to 375 degrees F. Serve plain or with Spanish Sauce. (See section on Savory Sauces.)

Dumplings

2 cups flour	½ teaspoon salt
4 teaspoons baking powder	3 tablespoons Nucoa
¾ cup milk	

Mix the dry ingredients together and work in the Nucoa with the back and edge of a spoon. When flaky, add the milk and mix quickly. Turn onto a slightly floured board. Pat to one-half inch in thickness and cut in rounds of the desired size. Place in the boiling liquid. Cover closely and steam fifteen minutes.

Dumpling Stew

Prepare veal, lamb, beef, chicken or fish stew according to the usual recipe. When boiling hard, place the dumplings on the stew, cover closely and steam fifteen minutes.

Layer Dumpling Stew

Prepare any kind of meat stew according to the usual recipe. Leave a thin layer in the kettle; be sure it is boiling. On this put a layer of tiny dumplings. Cover with several inches of stew. Then put in a second layer of dumplings. Pour in more stew, put in more dumplings, cover closely and boil for fifteen minutes.

SIZZLING PLATTERS

There's something new in the world—sizzling platters! Enter New York's smart restaurants. Your ears are greeted by a sound like swarming bees. Waiters dash hither and yon with great metal platters, sizzling and sputtering, puffing savory whiffs like volcanic eruptions into the air!

It's the latest way of cooking and serving, of keeping foods piping hot on their travels from stove to table. A whole meal, crackling and seasoned to a turn, is arranged on a single sizzling hot metal or fireproof platter.

To adapt this innovation to home equipment, choose foods that will not dry out when in contact with the hot dish; for instance, a broiled lamb chop, sausage, and a kidney; stuffed baked potato and grilled tomato. Or you could use pan-broiled meat patties, seasoned with tomato and onion juice; Simplified French Fried Onion Rings and Parslied Potatoes. Supplement these sizzling platters with a thin soup, add a salad and a light dessert, and the meal is made.

And to make broiled foods the grand success this type of service demands, baste them freely with melted New Nucoa during the cooking; and just before serving, spread with Nucoa, colored golden, and slip the platter for a moment into the oven.

Broiled Minute Hamburgs

Order one and a half pounds of round steak put through the chopper. Add a half-teaspoon salt, mix well, and pat into flat cakes a half-inch thick. Rub a fine-meshed broiler or a pan with Nucoa and place the hamburgs on it. Broil for eight minutes, turning once. Then dust with salt and pepper, dot with Nucoa, colored golden, reheat a moment and serve sizzling hot.

Broiled Lamb Patties

Order one and a half pounds of tender raw lamb put through the chopper. Add a half teaspoon salt, mix and shape into round cakes a half-inch thick. With a toothpick fasten a slice of bacon around each patty. Rub a fine-meshed broiler or a pan with Nucoa; place the patties on it and broil eight to ten minutes, first on one side, then the other. Season with salt and pepper, dot with Nucoa, colored golden, reheat and serve sizzling hot.

CHICKEN DINNERS

Fowls are to the kitchen, says Brillat-Savarin, what canvas is to the painter. They are served up boiled, roasted, fried, hot or cold, whole or in pieces, with or without sauce, boned, skinned or stuffed and always with equal success!

And this burst of praise from a French gourmet is hardly an exaggeration, for chicken has been a festive dish in every land from the time of the Greek ceremonial feasts, down to our own American plantation days when a young chicken was invariably a sacrificial offering to company.

The first and best meal in any port is almost sure to be chicken, whether it's Chinese chow mein, Austrian Bakhuhn, or Poulet de Bresse. The whole world has contributed its secrets of chicken cookery; in this book we've adapted them to American methods and American ingredients. The recipes are short, easy to remember, and make it possible to create a luxury flavor at an economy cost. And here's how—

Before roasting chicken, rub it all over with a paste of equal parts of flour and the New Nucoa.

When broiling, baste with melted New Nucoa.

When frying, use the New Nucoa, and at that only enough to cover the bottom of the pan. The result—delicacy of flavor, a golden brown richness of color and tenderness supreme.

ALL MEASUREMENTS ARE LEVEL

Fried Chicken

2 (2 pound) frying chickens	Nucoa
Flour	Salt and pepper

Order the chicken disjointed and cut up as for fricassee. Wash. Drain until dry. Dust with salt and pepper and roll each piece in flour. In a warm heavy frying pan melt enough Nucoa to insure a depth of a scant one-half inch. In this slowly fry the chicken turning only once. It should brown in about twenty minutes. Then dot with a little extra

Nucoa, cover closely and place in a moderately hot oven, 350-375 degrees F. for twenty minutes longer or steam it for forty-five minutes. Either method will make it very tender. The chicken may be served with a gravy made from the drippings in the frying pan. In this case pour out all but two tablespoons of the Nucoa. Stir in two tablespoons of flour and slowly add one and one-half cups of thin cream or rich hot milk, or use water if brown gravy is desired. Fried Chicken may also be served with Bêchamel or Brown Mushroom Sauce. (See section on Savory Sauces.)

Baked Maryland Chicken

2 (2 pound) broiling or frying chickens	Flour
Nucoa	Salt pork or bacon
Salt and pepper	Hot Water
	Medium Thick White Cream Sauce
Corn Fritters	

Order the chicken disjointed as for fricassee. Wash. Drain until well dried and roll each piece in melted Nucoa. Dust with a little salt and pepper. Then roll in flour and place, skin side up, in a dripping pan well rubbed with Nucoa. Place a small strip of salt pork or bacon on each piece of chicken. Put in a very hot oven, 420-425 degrees F., and when the flour begins to brown, add a half cup of hot water and baste the chicken every ten minutes with the pan drippings. When the chicken is well browned, cover and cook until tender, from forty-five minutes to an hour. Serve with the Medium Thick White Cream Sauce poured around it; and garnish with the Corn Fritters.

Bakhuhn

2 (2 pound) frying chickens, cleaned and dressed	8 tablespoons flour
3 eggs	¾ teaspoon salt
	2 cups fine sifted dry bread crumbs
Nucoa for frying (1 pound)	

Beat the eggs; add the flour and salt; and beat the mixture until smooth. Singe, wash and dry the chicken, and cut in quarters. Dip the chicken in the egg mixture; then in the crumbs. Heat the Nucoa in a heavy iron frying pan until it starts to bubble; put in the chicken; and fry slowly over a moderate heat until browned and tender throughout. Turn the chicken once during the cooking. Allow from twelve to fifteen minutes for quartered chicken, and from twenty to thirty for a small whole chicken.

Poulet de Bresse
(French Chicken Casserole)

1. With tender broiling or frying chickens, order three small chickens for six people. Have them split and dressed. Wash and dry and place in a good-sized casserole thickly rubbed with Nucoa. Dust the chicken with salt and pepper and dot with three tablespoons Nucoa. Cover closely and roast in a hot oven, 400 degrees F. from thirty to thirty-five minutes.

2. With a roasting chicken, follow the same directions using a three- or four-pound roasting chicken with this exception: Put a little Nucoa inside the bird and roast it for an hour and a quarter to an hour and a half turning once during the process. It should be laid breast down when started.

3. With a fowl, follow the preceding directions, putting a tablespoonful of minced onion and a cup of chopped celery in the casserole. Allow from two to two and a half hours for the cookery. Lower the oven temperature at the end of thirty minutes.

Russian Chicken Pie

Short Biscuit Meat Pie Pastry or Quick Puff Paste	3 cups good-sized pieces cooked chicken
Béchamel Sauce	1 cup shredded sautéd mushrooms

Prepare the pastry. Roll to one-fourth inch in thickness; fit over a large inverted layer-cake pan and prick in several places to allow the air to escape. Bake in a hot oven, 375 degrees F., until browned, about twenty minutes. Roll out the trimmings from the pastry to one-fourth inch in thickness and cut them into fancy shapes. Bake this to use in ornamenting the top of the pie. While the crust is baking, prepare the Béchamel Sauce and sauté the mushrooms in a little Nucoa. Add the chicken and mushrooms to the sauce. Let stand ten minutes over boiling water to become very hot; just before serving put it into the pie-shell and decorate with the figures of cooked pastry. (For pastry recipes see Index.)

Hungarian Paprika Chicken with Noodles

3 cups cooked chicken, cut in large pieces	Medium Thick White Cream Sauce or Béchamel Sauce
	Noodles

Heat the chicken in the sauce. Serve with boiled noodles, garnish with carrots, coarse crumbs of bread fried golden in a little Nucoa and with a thick dusting of paprika.

Bread Stuffing

(For chicken, turkey, duck or fish)

2 cups soft bread crumbs	1½ teaspoons poultry seasoning
¼ cup Nucoa, melted	1 tablespoon finely minced onion
¾ teaspoon salt	½ tablespoon minced parsley (optional)
¼ teaspoon pepper	Boiling water

Combine the ingredients in the order given and moisten sparingly with the boiling water.

DESSERTS AND SWEET SAUCES

The word *dessert,* it is said, came originally from a French verb meaning *to clear away.* Whether a correct derivation or not, epicures soon discovered that a cleared table was merely a setting for the real triumph of the meal, and glorious puddings, exquisite cakes, and rare fruits soon made their appearance as the climax of lunch or dinner.

The perfect dessert is a masterpiece, supplementing the more serious courses. If they are rich and heavy, the dessert must be light and mildly acid—as a pomme bonne femme (baked apple) or a Viennese fruit tart. If the other courses are light, the dessert should be substantial, as an English steamed raisin pudding, or a Russian sour cream cake.

But whatever the dessert, it must be tempting to the sight and delicious to the taste. The sauce must be temptingly fragrant, and of creamy smoothness. The New Nucoa gives the superb texture, richness, and delicacy of flavor demanded by gourmets everywhere, in their desserts, but at an economy price.

ALL MEASUREMENTS ARE LEVEL

Raisin Roll Pudding

2 cups flour	4 tablespoons Nucoa
4 teaspoons baking powder	¾ cup milk
½ teaspoon salt	2 additional tablespoons Nucoa
1 tablespoon sugar	¾ cup raisins
	¼ cup sugar (additional)

Sift together the flour, baking powder, salt and the one tablespoon sugar. Chop in the four tablespoons Nucoa with the back and edge of a spoon, keeping the mixture flaky. Moisten with the milk. Roll into an oblong shape one-half inch in thickness; spread with the remaining Nucoa; dot with the raisins; and sprinkle with the sugar. Roll as for jelly roll, pinching the ends together. Place, fold side down, in a steamer rubbed with Nucoa and steam for fifty minutes. Serve with Hard or Pineapple Sauce.

Pineapple Sauce

¾ cup diced canned pineapple	½ cup sugar
1 cup pineapple juice	1 lemon, sliced
1 cup boiling water	2 tablespoons Nucoa
Juice 1 lemon	2 tablespoons flour
Few grains nutmeg	

Combine pineapple, pineapple juice, water, lemon juice, sugar and lemon slices; boil five minutes; stir in the Nucoa, creamed with the flour; stir until boiling point is reached; and flavor with nutmeg.

Hard Sauce

½ cup Nucoa, colored golden	2 cups confectioners' sugar (sifted)
1 tablespoon boiling water, or sherry	½ teaspoon vanilla (if sherry is not used)

Stir the Nucoa until creamy. Gradually work in the water or sherry and the sugar. Beat until very creamy. Heap in a dish and chill until firm.

Baked Apple or Apricot Charlotte

1 small loaf of bread (24 hours old)	1 teaspoon cinnamon
½ cup melted Nucoa	Juice of ½ lemon
3 cups apple sauce or stewed apricots	Marmalade

Rub a medium-sized mould with Nucoa and line with strips of the bread, from which the crust should be removed. The bread should be moistened with the Nucoa. Put in a layer of the sauce, well sweetened and flavored with the cinnamon and lemon juice. Over this put a layer of the Nucoa-d bread. Continue until all is used, making the last layer bread. Bake until golden brown in a hot oven, 375 degrees F. Turn onto a fire-proof plate. Cover with marmalade. Return to the oven for a moment or two; and serve hot or cold with cream.

Steamed French Bread Pudding

1 small loaf bread	¼ teaspoon nutmeg
¼ cup Nucoa	Grated rind 1 orange
1 cup sugar	½ teaspoon baking powder
2 eggs	⅓ cup chopped raisins
2 tablespoons shredded citron (optional)	

The bread should be cut or broken in very small pieces. (Or use three cups, solidly packed, bread cubes.) Barely cover it with hot water; cool and press as much water out as possible. Cream the

Nucoa with the sugar and the egg yolks, slightly beaten. Add the bread, nutmeg, orange rind, baking powder, raisins and citron. Fold in the egg whites, stiffly whipped. Transfer to a mould rubbed with Nucoa. Cover closely, and steam for two hours. Unmould and serve with Hard or Pineapple Sauce.

Rolled Bread Crumb Jam Cakes

1 cup fine dry bread crumbs	½ teaspoon salt
2½ cups sour milk or buttermilk	1 tablespoon sugar
10 tablespoons flour	1 egg well beaten
1 teaspoon baking powder	1 teaspoon Nucoa, melted
½ teaspoon baking soda	Nucoa for frying

Jam or Marmalade

Combine the crumbs and milk and let stand thirty minutes; then add the remaining dry ingredients sifted together; beat well; stir in the beaten egg and the melted Nucoa. Thoroughly oil a griddle or heavy iron frying pan with Nucoa. Drop the cake mixture by tablespoonsful on the griddle. When bubbly on one side, turn to brown the other. Spread the cakes as soon as fried with a little Nucoa, creamed with four times the quantity of jam or marmalade. Roll up and serve with confectioners' or powdered sugar sifted over the top.

In making these for a good-sized family, roll the cakes as soon as finished and place them, not touching, in rows in a pan slightly rubbed with Nucoa. Place this in the oven and just before serving, sift the sugar over them. They will stand for ten or fifteen minutes.

Sweet Biscuit Short Cakes

3 cups flour	¾ teaspoon salt
5 teaspoons baking powder	½ cup Nucoa
2 tablespoons sugar	1⅛ cups milk

Prepared sweetened fruit

Mix the dry ingredients together. Work in the Nucoa with the back and edge of a spoon; when flaky slowly add the milk. Transfer to a slightly floured board, and pat out to one-half inch in thickness. Shape into three-inch rounds with a biscuit cutter; place in a pan rubbed slightly with Nucoa and bake in a hot oven, 375-400 degrees F. until brown and puffy, about twenty minutes. Split while hot. Spread with Nucoa and put together and top with the prepared fruit. Serve garnished with sweetened whipped cream, or accompanied by Hard Sauce.

Strawberry Short Cakes

Wash and hull one quart of strawberries; reserve a few large berries for garnishing. Slice the remaining berries; add sugar to sweeten, about one-half cup; set aside for half an hour to start the juices. Split the shortcake biscuits and complete as described in the recipe for Sweet Biscuit Shortcakes. Garnish each serving with a whole strawberry.

Russian Peach, Apple or Plum Cake

½ cup Nucoa	½ teaspoon cinnamon
½ cup cream cheese	⅛ teaspoon ground clove
1½ cups cake flour	½ cup sifted powdered sugar
½ teaspoon salt	½ cup very thick sour cream

1½ cups peeled, sliced, good-sized peaches,
apples or small halved stoned plums

Measure the Nucoa into a mixing bowl; add the cheese and blend together. Then with a knife gradually and quickly work in the flour and salt. This makes a very thick paste. Transfer to a board dusted with flour and roll to a scant half-inch in thickness. Fit into a good-sized cake pan rubbed with Nucoa. Arrange the fruit in rows on the dough, pressing them slightly into it. Pour the sour cream over this and dust with the powdered sugar and spices. Bake in a hot oven, 375 degrees F. until the paste is tender. Allow about thirty-five minutes. Dust with additional sugar and serve.

Viennese Fruit Torte

1 cup cooked dry apricots or peaches	2 eggs
½ cup chopped walnuts, pecans,	1 cup sugar
hazelnuts or almonds	½ cup fine dry bread crumbs
¾ cup apricot or peach juice	¼ teaspoon salt
2 tablespoons Nucoa	2 teaspoons baking powder

½ cup raisins

Combine the fruits, nuts, fruit juice and Nucoa and simmer for ten minutes; then cool the mixture. Next, beat the eggs very light; add the sugar; then add the crumbs, salt and baking powder, mix together and add the raisins; stir in the cooked fruit mixture. Rub a medium-sized layer-cake pan with Nucoa and line with waxed paper. Spread the fruit torte mixture into this and bake in a moderate oven, 350 degrees F. for forty minutes. Cool. Serve plain or spread with a very thin layer of sweetened whipped cream and a sprinkling of chopped nut meats, shredded raisins, canned cherries or halved pistachios.

ICEBOX CAKES

Necessity has ever been the mother of invention. Some Russian house-wife coming downstairs one bitter winter morning, found her cream cake chilled—discovered on tasting that it was better than ever—and out of the night's freezing grew a new method of cookery.

America adapted it to modern refrigeration, and the icebox cake was born—the dessert calling for the richest of cream, and all in all the finest of ingredients. But this new dessert proved too expensive for the average purse until the New Nucoa was introduced to replace one of the most expensive ingredients and these luxury foods were brought within the reach of every purse.

ALL MEASUREMENTS ARE LEVEL

Russian Icebox Cake

2 squares (ounces) bitter chocolate ¼ cup granulated sugar
4 tablespoons Nucoa ¼ teaspoon vanilla
2 eggs ½ cup heavy cream
Lady fingers or strips of sponge cake

Melt the chocolate and the Nucoa together in the top of a double boiler. Separate the eggs and add the sugar to the yolks. Then beat until thick and lemon-colored. Gradually add to the chocolate mixture and beat until thick. Remove from the heat; add the vanilla and fold in the egg whites, beaten stiff and combined with the cream (also beaten stiff). Line a mould with lady fingers or strips of sponge cake and fill the center with the chocolate filling. Chill in the refrigerator an hour or two, or until the filling is firm. Unmould and serve garnished with whipped cream.

Hazelnut Icebox Cake

1 cup Nucoa, colored golden ⅓ cup orange juice
Grated rind 2 oranges 1 egg
2½ cups confectioners' sugar ½ cup finely chopped blanched hazelnuts
1½ teaspoons lemon juice Lady fingers or strips of sponge cake

73

Cream the Nucoa with the orange rind. Gradually work in the sugar and lemon and orange juice. Beat the egg until thick and lemon colored and beat into the Nucoa mixture with the hazelnuts. Transfer to a mould, lined with lady fingers or strips of sponge cake; chill in the refrigerator until the filling is firm. Serve with a garnish of sugared orange sections.

Butterscotch Icebox Cake

1 large round sponge cake	½ pint cream, whipped and sweetened
Butterscotch Filling	½ cup shredded salted almonds

Slice off the top of the sponge cake and scoop out the center portion, leaving a shell or wall of cake an inch and a half thick. Fill with the Butterscotch Filling; fit the top of the cake in place; cover with waxed paper; and chill over night in the refrigerator. When ready to use, transfer to a serving plate; cover the top and sides with the whipped cream; and stud all over with the shredded almonds.

Butterscotch Filling

1¼ cups dark brown sugar	¼ cup cold water
2 tablespoons Nucoa	2 eggs
1½ cups boiling water	¼ teaspoon salt
4 tablespoons flour	1 tablespoon lemon juice

Combine the brown sugar, Nucoa and boiling water in the top of a double boiler. Stir the flour, cold water, egg yolks and salt together to a smooth paste. Gradually add to the first mixture and cook and stir until thick. Remove from the heat and add the lemon juice. Cool slightly; and fold in the egg whites, stiffly whipped.

Seville Icebox Cake

1 cup Nucoa, colored golden	2 tablespoons cold strong coffee
2 cups confectioners' sugar	⅛ teaspoon cinnamon
3 tablespoons cocoa	2 eggs
Lady fingers or strips of sponge cake	

Cream the Nucoa. Gradually beat in one cup of the sugar, the cocoa, coffee and cinnamon. Beat the eggs until thick; and add to the first mixture with the remaining sugar. Beat with an egg beater until well blended. Line a mould with lady fingers or strips of sponge cake and fill with the Nucoa mixture. Chill in the refrigerator until the filling is firm. Unmould and serve plain or with a garnish of sweetened whipped cream.

CAKES

Cakes are among the pleasant discoveries of a culinary voyage through the Old World. In some sections, every town and village has its own special cake, distinguished by shape or flavor from every other cake of every other town. There are Dundee cakes, Savoy cakes, Genoa sponge cake. It's as if every small town baker were determined to spread abroad the name and fame of his town through the cake-ster's art.

But in truth, for all the hubbub these local bakers make about their specialties, there is no trick in cake making. Even the most veritable amateur can bake good cake, if she will abide by the rules. And here they are—

Measure level. Follow directions accurately. Use specified ingredients—cake flour, a reliable brand of baking powder, good flavorings, and above all, the right shortening.

But that question of the right shortening *is* important. It must be fresh and delicate in flavor. The New Nucoa meets that test with flying colors, made as it is from sweet pasteurized whole milk and pure American vegetable oils, then rushed by truck to dealers, and to you.

The right shortening ought to cream easily with the sugar. Nucoa does that. It creams at once in fact, and so saves valuable time in mixing.

The right shortening makes a cake that stays moist—and there again Nucoa scores. Cakes made with it stay fresh to the last crumb.

And finally, the right shortening makes rich cake at an economy cost. And the New Nucoa is again the answer!

ALL MEASUREMENTS ARE LEVEL

Economical Layer Cake

1 cup sugar	½ cup water
1 egg	1⅔ cups cake flour
½ cup Nucoa	½ teaspoon salt
1 teaspoon vanilla or other flavoring	2½ teaspoons baking powder

75

Stir the Nucoa, sugar, egg yolk and vanilla together until creamy. Sift together the dry ingredients and add alternately with the water to the first mixture. When well mixed stir in the egg white, stiffly whipped. Transfer to two nine-inch layer cake pans, which have been rubbed with Nucoa and dusted very lightly with flour. Bake about twenty-five minutes in a hot oven, 375 degrees F. When done, remove from the pans; cool; and put together with jam, jelly, any fruit butter, Italian Cream Filling, Creamy Icing or Rich Chocolate Icing. Or put the cake together just before serving with sweetened whipped cream or with sliced and sweetened oranges or other fruit.

Devil's Food Cake

2½ squares (ounces) bitter chocolate
½ cup Nucoa
1 cup sugar
½ teaspoon vanilla

1 large or 2 small eggs
1½ cups cake flour
2½ teaspoons baking powder
⅛ teaspoon salt

½ cup milk

Cut the chocolate in bits and melt it over hot water. Put it in a mixing bowl with the Nucoa, sugar, vanilla and lightly beaten egg yolk. Cream until very light. Sift together the dry ingredients and add them to the first mixture alternately with the milk. Fold in the egg white, stiffly beaten. Transfer to two eight-inch Nucoa-d layer-cake pans and bake twenty to twenty-five minutes in a moderately hot oven, 350 to 375 degrees F., or bake in a loaf pan allowing forty minutes. If made in the form of a layer cake, put together with Creamy or Rich Chocolate Icing or with sweetened whipped cream, flavored with a little melted chocolate. If made in a loaf, cover with either of the two icings and sprinkle thickly with chopped nuts, if desired.

Snow Cake

½ cup uncolored Nucoa
1 cup sugar
1½ tablespoons lemon juice
Grated rind ½ lemon

¼ teaspoon salt
2 cups cake flour
3 teaspoons baking powder
⅔ cup milk

3 egg whites

Put the Nucoa, sugar, lemon juice and rind in a bowl and cream until light and fluffy. Sift together the dry ingredients and add alternately to the mixture with the milk. Last, fold in the egg whites, stiffly beaten. Transfer to a good-sized cake pan rubbed with Nucoa. Make the mixture an inch deep. Bake in a hot oven, 375 degrees F.

about thirty-five minutes. Cool and cover with Orange or Uncooked Fudge Icing. (See section on Icings.)

Dundee Nut and Fruit Cake

⅔ cup granulated sugar
¾ cup Nucoa
3 eggs
3 tablespoons orange juice
2 cups cake flour
2 teaspoons baking powder
¼ teaspoon salt
1 teaspoon cinnamon

¼ teaspoon nutmeg
⅛ teaspoon clove
½ cup chopped nut meats, any kind
⅓ cup cleaned currants
½ cup chopped raisins
⅓ cup mixed chopped orange and
lemon peel and citron
Grated rind ½ orange
Grated rind 1 lemon

In a mixing bowl, put the sugar, Nucoa and the eggs, lightly beaten; and beat until creamy. Then add the orange juice. Sift together the dry ingredients; add all the nuts with the exception of two tablespoons which should be reserved. Stir in the fruits and the lemon and orange rind. When thoroughly mixed with the fruits, beat into the first mixture. It will be thick like a pound cake batter. Then transfer to an Angel-cake pan, which has been rubbed with Nucoa and lightly dusted with flour; sprinkle the remaining nuts over the top. Bake in a moderate oven, 350 degrees F. for an hour. Then turn upside down to cool on a cake rack. Keep closely covered in a jar or casserole for at least twenty-four hours before serving. This cake should not be iced.

Cornmeal Pound Cake

½ cup Nucoa
¾ cup sugar
2 eggs
1½ teaspoons baking powder
¼ teaspoon salt

½ teaspoon nutmeg
1¼ cups cornmeal, preferably finely
ground
½ cup cake flour
½ cup milk

Measure the Nucoa and sugar into a mixing bowl and beat until creamy. Add the eggs, lightly beaten. Mix together the dry ingredients and add alternately with the milk to the first mixture. Transfer to a good-sized Nucoa-d cake pan making the mixture about three-fourths of an inch deep. Bake in a moderately hot oven, 350-375 degrees F. for about thirty-five minutes. Cut in squares and serve hot or cold.

Two-Egg Cake

⅔ cup Nucoa
1 cup sugar
2 medium-sized eggs
1 teaspoon vanilla

1¾ cups cake flour
2 teaspoons baking powder
½ teaspoon salt
½ cup milk

Stir the Nucoa until creamy and gradually work in the sugar. Slightly beat the eggs; add the vanilla; combine with the Nucoa mixture and blend. Sift the dry ingredients together and add alternately with the milk to the first mixture. Transfer to two nine-inch layer-cake pans rubbed with Nucoa and dusted sparingly with flour. Bake in a moderate oven, 375 degrees F. for twenty-five minutes, or until firm in the center and brown on top. Remove from the pans; cool and put together and cover with the desired frosting.

Hungarian Chocolate Cake

Follow the preceding recipe; baking the cake in four (seven- or eight-inch) layer cake pans. Cool and put together and cover with the Rich Chocolate Icing in this book. Decorate the top of the cake with shaved walnuts.

French Petit Fours
or
Little Bridge Cakes

Follow the recipe for Two-Egg Cake. Transfer the batter to a shallow oblong pan rubbed with Nucoa and dusted sparingly with flour. Bake in a moderate oven, 375 degrees F. for thirty minutes, or until firm in the center and brown on top. Remove from the pan and cool. Cut into small squares, round and diamond-shaped pieces. Brush off the crumbs and cover the top and sides with the Creamy Icing or Rich Chocolate Icing in this book. Decorate each cake with small candies, chopped nuts, candied fruits or icing forced through a very small pastry tube.

Italian Cream Cake

Follow the recipe for Two-Egg Cake baking it in two layers. Put together with Italian Cream Filling and top with a thick layer of quince jam, which should be sprinkled thickly with chopped nutmeats of any kind. Place closely covered in a refrigerator for a few hours before serving.

Apricot or Prune Cake Loaf

½ cup Nucoa
1 cup sugar
2 eggs
1½ cups cake flour
½ teaspoon baking powder
⅓ teaspoon salt
1 teaspoon baking soda

1 teaspoon cinnamon
½ teaspoon cloves
½ teaspoon nutmeg
¼ cup sour milk
1 cup cooked, chopped, drained, pitted prunes or stewed dried apricots

Cream the Nucoa; gradually work in the sugar; beat until blended. Add the eggs, slightly beaten. Sift the dry ingredients; and add alternately with the milk to the first mixture. Add the chopped prunes or apricots; and beat until well mixed. Transfer to a shallow loaf cake pan rubbed with Nucoa and dusted with flour; and bake in a moderate oven, 350 degrees F. for forty-five minutes or until the cake is brown and firm in the center. Remove from the pan and cool. Serve hot as a dessert with Hard Sauce or lemon sauce, or replace in the pan topside up; and spread with Creamy Icings. (See Icing Section.) Allow the icing to harden; and mark in squares for serving.

Chocolate Shadow Cakes

2½ squares (ounces) bitter chocolate
1 egg
½ cup milk
1 cup sugar
2 tablespoons Nucoa
¾ teaspoon baking soda

½ teaspoon vanilla
1 cup and 2 tablespoons cake flour
⅛ teaspoon salt
½ teaspoon cinnamon
½ cup milk (additional)

Cut the chocolate in bits and melt it over hot water; separate the egg; beat the white until stiff and the yolk until creamy. Add the yolk to the first half cupful of milk and stir into the melted chocolate; cook and stir until it thickens. Add this to the sugar and Nucoa which should be in a bowl. Add the vanilla, flour, salt and cinnamon sifted together, and the remaining milk. Dissolve the soda in a teaspoon of boiling water and add to the cake mixture; fold in the egg white. Transfer to a medium-sized shallow Nucoa-d cake pan dusted with flour and bake forty minutes in a moderate oven, 350 degrees F. Cool; when absolutely cold, cut in squares and cover with the Shadow Icing in this book.

CAKE ICINGS

There is a little French woman in New York who has made a career of wedding cakes. Creations of icy towers and battlements! Wedding bells and garlands! Brides and grooms clasping sugary hands!

Not everyone aspires to icings like that, but rich moist icings—smooth as the poet Keats' creamy curd—ought to be in every cook's repertoire.

They can be, too, if home cake bakers will take a leaf from the notebooks of makers of sweet biscuits. These expert bakers are using the New Nucoa as an ingredient for the fillings of their choicest biscuits; they have found that Nucoa supplies a richness of flavor obtainable in no other way—at a minimum cost.

Here are recipes for some of the smart new icings as seen in Fifth Avenue shops. Spread them smoothly on the cold cake by means of a supple knife dipped in hot water, if you wish to decorate the cake afterwards. Spread them nonchalantly and thickly in swirls if you are a devotee of thick icing. If more ambitious still, squeeze them through a pastry bag and tubes into ornamental designs.

ALL MEASUREMENTS ARE LEVEL

Orange Icing

2 tablespoons Nucoa	Few grains salt
1 egg yolk	Confectioners' sugar to spread, about
1½ tablespoons orange juice	2 cups
½ tablespoon lemon juice	

Stir the Nucoa and egg yolks together until creamy and add a little of the confectioners' sugar which should be sifted. Then alternately add fruit juice and confectioners' sugar until all has been used. Beat thoroughly with each addition.

Rich Six-Minute Icing

1 tablespoon Nucoa	3 tablespoons boiling water
1 cup sugar	½ teaspoon baking powder
1 egg white	½ teaspoon vanilla

Melt the Nucoa in the top of a double boiler; add the sugar, egg white and water; place over hot water. Then bring to a boil. Cook and beat continually with a rotary egg beater for six minutes. Remove from the heat; beat in the vanilla and baking powder and continue to beat until stiff enough to spread on the cake, which should be cold.

Creamy Icing

¼ cup Nucoa   1 teaspoon vanilla
2 cups sifted confectioners' sugar   ⅛ teaspoon salt
2 tablespoons hot milk

Cream the Nucoa; and gradually work in one cup of the confectioners' sugar, vanilla and salt; add the hot milk. Add the second cup of confectioners' sugar; and beat until creamy.

Rich Chocolate Icing

4 tablespoons Nucoa   1 cup confectioners' sugar
4 squares bitter chocolate   ⅔ cup light cream or undiluted
⅛ teaspoon salt   evaporated milk
1 teaspoon vanilla

Combine the Nucoa and chocolate in the top of a double boiler; and melt over hot water. Remove from the heat; add the remaining ingredients; beat with a rotary egg beater until the icing is thick enough to spread.

Shadow Icing

I	II
2 tablespoons hot milk	2 squares bitter chocolate, shaved
¼ cup Nucoa	3 tablespoons boiling water
2 cups sifted confectioners' sugar	2 tablespoons granulated sugar
1 teaspoon vanilla	
⅛ teaspoon salt	

Put the hot milk into a small bowl; add the Nucoa and gradually work in the confectioners' sugar, vanilla and salt to form a creamy icing; spread this on the cake. When firm, pour over it a shadow topping. Make this topping by combining the melted chocolate with the water and granulated sugar, and bringing all to a rapid boil. Cool until tepid and pour over the firm creamy icing. When poured over the cake, it will run down the sides in shadow-like streaks.

Uncooked Fudge Icing

2 squares (ounces) melted bitter   1 tablespoon top cream
    chocolate   ½ teaspoon vanilla
2 tablespoons Nucoa
    Sifted confectioners' sugar to spread, about 2 cups

Melt the chocolate in a small pan; remove from the heat; transfer to a bowl; and stir in the cream, Nucoa, vanilla, and a half cup of the sugar. Then beat in the remaining sugar, using a little additional sugar if the icing is to be stiff.

Italian Cream Filling

1 cup milk   1 egg
⅓ cup sugar   ¼ teaspoon salt
¼ cup flour   ½ teaspoon vanilla or 1 tablespoon rum

Scald the milk; combine the flour and a fourth cup extra milk; and mix to a smooth paste—stir into the scalded milk. Cook and stir until thickened. Beat the egg; add the sugar and salt and pour into the thickened milk. Cook for ten minutes longer, stirring occasionally, and then add the flavoring.

COOKIES

Tea time in an old garden overlooking the River Thames. Far below boats floating lazily with the current. Under the spreading trees, little tables set with blue china. Plates heaped high with cookies—cookies with caraway and raisins, crisp rich squares delicately flavored. What matter if English cooks simply call them biscuits—to us they are all cookies.

But what hours of time have gone into their making! Far too many for efficiency-loving Americans. That's why we scurried all over the world to discover easier methods—to describe to you in this book. We finally found the idea in Russia and Scandinavia, where women chill the cookie dough. Just a step from that to time-saving delicious icebox cookies. Made of the proper ingredients, the dough keeps fresh in the refrigerator for weeks, and crisp cookies newly baked can be served every day.

Proper ingredients are essential—that means first of all the right shortening—rich and easy to mix, a shortening that tastes and keeps fresh. The New Nucoa meets every requirement. It is the ideal shortening for these new cookies with the old-time quality.

ALL MEASUREMENTS ARE LEVEL

English Tea Cookies

4½ cups cake flour	3 eggs
3 teaspoons baking powder	¼ teaspoon nutmeg
⅓ teaspoon salt	1 teaspoon vanilla
1 cup Nucoa	1½ cups powdered sugar
1 cup milk	

Sift the flour, baking powder and salt together. Work in the Nucoa with the finger tips until the mixture looks flaky. Beat the eggs until thick; add the nutmeg, vanilla and sugar and combine with the milk. Add to the first mixture; and beat until smooth and free from lumps. Drop by large teaspoonsful on shallow pans or cooky sheets rubbed with Nucoa. Dust with a little additional powdered sugar and nutmeg

83

combined; and bake in a hot oven—375 degrees F. for twelve minutes, or until brown on top.

Dropped Hermits

½ cup Nucoa
1 cup brown sugar
2 eggs, well beaten
¼ teaspoon baking soda
2 tablespoons sour milk
1 cup flour
⅓ teaspoon salt
¼ teaspoon nutmeg
½ teaspoon cloves
¾ cup chopped raisins
Additional flour—about one and one-half cups

Cream the Nucoa; and gradually work in the sugar. Add the eggs, and the soda and sour milk combined. Beat until blended. Sift the first cup of flour with the salt and spices; and add the raisins. Add to the first mixture; and beat in enough sifted flour to make the dough stiff enough to hold its shape—about one and a half cupsful. Drop by teaspoonful on a shallow pan or cooky sheet rubbed with Nucoa; and bake in a moderate oven—350 degrees F. for twelve minutes, or until brown on top.

Old-Fashioned Molasses Raisin Cookies

½ cup Nucoa
½ cup light brown sugar
1 egg
⅔ cup molasses
3½ cups cake flour
½ teaspoon salt
1 teaspoon cloves
1 teaspoon cinnamon
1 teaspoon nutmeg
¾ cup chopped raisins
½ cup sour milk
½ teaspoon baking soda

Cream the Nucoa; and gradually work in the sugar. Add the egg, slightly beaten, and the molasses. Beat until blended. Sift together all the dry ingredients except the baking soda and add the raisins. Combine the sour milk and baking soda; and add alternately with the dry ingredients to the first mixture. Drop by teaspoonful on a shallow pan or cooky sheet rubbed with Nucoa, and bake in a moderate oven 350 degrees F. for fifteen minutes, or until firm in the center.

Swedish Icebox Cookies

1 cup Nucoa
1 cup light brown sugar
2 eggs
3 cups cake flour
¼ teaspoon baking soda
1 teaspoon baking powder
⅓ teaspoon salt
¾ teaspoon cinnamon
¼ teaspoon ground clove
½ cup finely chopped almonds

Stir the Nucoa until creamy; gradually work in the sugar and add the eggs, well beaten. Sift the dry ingredients together and combine with the first mixture. Form into a roll two inches in diameter; wrap in waxed paper and chill a few hours or until firm enough to slice. Then slice paper thin. Transfer to a cooky sheet rubbed with Nucoa and sprinkle the tops with the almonds. Bake in a hot oven, 375 degrees F. for ten minutes or until a delicate brown.

Coconut Cookies

Follow the directions for Swedish Icebox Cookies, omitting the spices and almonds. Flavor with a teaspoon of vanilla. Chill and slice; sprinkle the cookies with two-thirds cup shredded coconut and bake as directed.

Chocolate Wafers

½ cup Nucoa
2½ squares (ounces) bitter chocolate
  (melted)
⅔ cup granulated sugar
½ teaspoon salt
2 eggs
½ teaspoon vanilla
2 cups cake flour
1 teaspoon baking powder

Cream the Nucoa; add the chocolate and blend. Gradually beat in the sugar; and add the vanilla and eggs, slightly beaten. Sift the dry ingredients; and add to the first mixture. Form into two rolls. Wrap in waxed paper and chill in the refrigerator for a few hours or until firm enough to slice. Slice paper thin. Transfer to a cooky sheet rubbed with Nucoa and bake in a moderate oven, 375 degrees F. for ten minutes or until firm in the center.

Fruit and Nut Icebox Wafers

1½ cups Nucoa
1½ cups granulated sugar
1 egg
1 egg yolk
Grated rind ½ orange
½ cup finely chopped walnuts
  or pecans
½ cup finely chopped dates
2½ cups cake flour
1 tablespoon orange juice

Cream the Nucoa and gradually work in the sugar. Add the egg and the egg yolk, beaten until thick. Combine the grated orange rind, nuts, dates and flour; and add with the orange juice to the first mixture. Form into two rolls; wrap in waxed paper and chill a few hours in the refrigerator until firm. Cut in thin slices; transfer to a cooky sheet rubbed with Nucoa; and bake in a moderate oven, 375 degrees F. for ten minutes.

Chinese Almond Cakes

4 cups cake flour	⅓ teaspoon salt
1 cup sugar	1 cup Nucoa
½ teaspoon baking powder	5 eggs

Blanched almonds

Sift the dry ingredients together in a bowl. Work in the Nucoa with finger tips as in making pie crust; add the eggs; and beat until the mixture is thoroughly blended. Place by teaspoonful in little smooth mounds on a cooky sheet or pan rubbed with Nucoa. Put a blanched almond in the center of each. Bake in a moderate oven, 350-375 degrees F. until browned, from twelve to fifteen minutes.

Scotch Oat Cakes

1 pound rolled oats	3 teaspoons baking powder
¾ cup cake flour	1 teaspoon salt
3 tablespoons sugar	½ cup Nucoa

Milk to moisten

Put the oatmeal through the food chopper. Then mix with the flour, baking powder, salt and sugar. Add the Nucoa and rub together with the hands until smooth. Heap up the mixture; make a hole in the center. Pour in slowly just enough milk to make a thick paste the consistency of pie crust. Place by tablespoonful on a floured board and roll into thin rounds (not more than an eighth-inch thick). Cut each in quarters. Place on greased pans; bake in a moderate oven, 350 degrees F. until a pale brown. These resemble oatmeal crackers.

PIES AND TARTS

Sunday morning in Paris. Bakers' windows gleaming. Rows upon rows of tarts. Tiny tarts that make a crisp mouthful. Middle-sized tarts just right for a twosome. And great big tarts for the whole family. Succulent whole fruits in flaky pastry shells—plums, cherries, strawberries, slices of apple and peachlike flower petals, all glazed over with rich jelly. Huge squares of *flan,* the thick custard pie loved by country folk.

Wherever the traveller goes, it's the same story. The whole world loves pie! In England, it's juicy gooseberry and apple tart with clotted Devonshire cream; in Vienna, rich flaky apple strudel; in America, foamy lemon meringue, pumpkin and butterscotch pie.

What's the secret of their goodness? The crust. And what makes the crust good? Proper handling, and the best of ingredients. How well they know that abroad! How carefully the French cook chooses his shortening! How lightly he works! No chilling of the pastry, no using ice water, no special mixer or board—his method is simplicity itself.

In the recipes in this book, we have adapted the foreign pastry cook's methods to American needs, using the very best shortening—the New Nucoa. Its delicacy of flavor, its perfection of texture, insures a rich, flaky crust, easily and quickly made.

ALL MEASUREMENTS ARE LEVEL

Plain Pie Crust

2 cups cake flour	½ teaspoon baking powder
½ teaspoon salt	⅔ cup Nucoa
Cold water (about 4 tablespoons)	

Sift together the dry ingredients. Add the Nucoa and chop it in with the back and edge of a spoon until the mixture is like coarse bran. Then lightly mix in the water using a fork; add only four tablespoonsful of water and just enough extra, if necessary, to make

87

a dough of the consistency to roll. Take up the paste with the floured hands and press it lightly together. (It should be kept as dry as possible.) Place on a lightly floured board and with a floured rolling pin, roll it to an eighth of an inch in thickness. This makes enough crust for a medium-sized two-crust pie and one pie-crust shell or a few tart shells. The dough may be wrapped in waxed paper and kept in the refrigerator for a week or so if desired.

Rich Short Pie Crust
(For pies of all kinds)

2 cups cake flour	½ teaspoon salt
2 teaspoons powdered sugar	¾ cup Nucoa
½ teaspoon baking powder	1 egg yolk, slightly beaten
6 tablespoons cold water	

Measure the flour, sugar, baking powder and salt into a medium-sized chopping bowl. Add the Nucoa and chop it lightly in until the flakes are the size of fairly large flakes of bran. Add the egg yolk and cold water and mix lightly with the flaked mixture. The pastry should barely stick together. Roll and use for any kind of pie. It is not necessary to chill this pastry.

Sweet Tart Pastry
(For tarts and fruit pies)

2 cups cake flour	Grated rind ½ lemon
½ cup powdered sugar	2 egg yolks
⅓ teaspoon salt	¾ cup Nucoa
6 tablespoons cold water	

Sift together the flour, sugar and salt into a mixing bowl. Make a well in the center; into this put the lemon rind, egg yolks and the Nucoa. Mix with a knife until the Nucoa is distributed in flakes as large as corn flakes. Then gradually mix in the cold water. If not sufficiently moist, carefully add a little more water. Roll out and use for tarts when a sweet crust is desired.

Quick Puff Paste
(For patty shells, rich meat pies and French pastry)

2 cups cake flour	½ teaspoon lemon juice
⅓ teaspoon salt	1 tablespoon cold water
1 cup Nucoa	6 tablespoons cold water (additional)

Sift the flour and salt onto a small moulding board. Cut the Nucoa into bits the size of filberts and lightly mix into the flour. Heap up this mixture making a well in the center. Into this put the lemon juice and the tablespoon of cold water; mix lightly leaving the bits of Nucoa whole. Then gradually add the remaining cold water until a fairly soft paste has been formed. Scrape off the moulding board and flour it lightly. Transfer the dough to the moulding board; dust it with a very little flour and quickly and lightly roll it into a long strip. Fold over in three equal parts pressing the edges together. Then turn around so the folded edges will be at the right and left and roll out as before. Repeat this rolling four times, when the paste will be ready to use.

Butterscotch Pie

Rich Short Pie Crust
1 cup old-fashioned dark brown sugar
3 tablespoons Nucoa
1½ cups milk

½ teaspoon vanilla
2 eggs
3 tablespoons flour
2 tablespoons powdered sugar

Roll out the pie crust to one-eighth of an inch in thickness. Cover an inverted pie plate with it and prick in several places to allow the air to escape. Bake until golden in a hot oven, 375-400 degrees F., to form a pie-crust shell. Then measure the sugar and Nucoa together into a heavy frying pan, slightly heated, caramelizing them together (that is, cooking them together until a thick brown syrup is formed.) To this add one cup of milk and the vanilla. Separate the eggs; beat the yolks lightly and combine with the remaining milk and the flour, beaten together until smooth. Pour this into the caramelized mixture and stir until thick and creamy. Pour this into the baked pie-crust shell. Cover with a meringue made by beating the egg whites until stiff with the powdered sugar. Place in a very slow oven, 325 degrees F., and bake until the meringue is browned, about ten minutes. Serve cold.

Apple Cream Pie

Thick apple sauce   Rich Short Pie Crust
Italian Cream Filling (recipe in Icing section)
Meringue

Make Rich Short Pie Crust; roll it to one-eighth inch thickness; fit it over an inverted pie-plate; prick around the edges to let the air escape; and bake twelve minutes in a hot oven, 400 degrees F. Cool; and just before serving put in the Italian Cream Fillng. Top with a layer of apple sauce; and cover with a meringue made by beating two egg whites until stiff, and adding two tablespoons powdered sugar. Place the pie in a slow oven, 325 degrees F., and cook the meringue twelve minutes.

French Custard Pie
(A modified 'Flan')

Rich Short Pie Crust	½ teaspoon vanilla
3 eggs	2 cups milk
½ cup granulated sugar	¼ cup granulated sugar (additional)
¼ teaspoon salt	4 tablespoons boiling water

Line a nine-inch plate with the pastry and build up the edges snugly to the edge of the plate. Prick slightly in several places; put in a very hot oven, 400-425 degrees F. and bake six minutes. In the meanwhile, separate the eggs; combine the yolks with one-half cup sugar and one-quarter teaspoon salt and vanilla and beat until thick. Add the milk and fold in the stiffly beaten egg whites. Pour this mixture into the partly baked crust and bake thirty minutes in a slower oven, 350-375 degrees F., or until a knife when inserted in the center comes out clean. Pour a caramelized glaze over the top of the pie. Cool and serve.

Note: To make the glaze, melt one-fourth cup granulated sugar in a small frying pan; add the boiling water and cook until a little forms a thread when dropped from a spoon.

Peach or Apple Strudel

3 tablespoons Nucoa	½ cup chopped raisins
1⅓ cups flour	½ cup chopped almonds (optional)
¼ teaspoon salt	½ cup sugar
3 tablespoons milk	¼ cup Nucoa (additional)
1 egg	1 cup fine dry bread crumbs
2 cups finely chopped, peeled apples or peaches	1 teaspoon cinnamon

Sift the flour and salt together; and work in the Nucoa with a knife until flaky. Combine the milk and the egg, well beaten; and add to the first mixture. Work with a spoon to form a soft dough. Combine the apples, raisins, almonds, sugar, cinnamon and the bread crumbs, browned in the fourth cup of Nucoa. Transfer the dough to a board dusted with flour; and roll as thin as possible into rectangular shape. Spread with the prepared apple mixture; and lightly press the filling into the dough with the rolling pin. Roll the strudel up like jelly roll; and transfer to a shallow pan, generously rubbed with Nucoa. Bake in a moderate oven, 350-375 degrees F. for forty minutes, basting twice during the baking with a little melted Nucoa. Serve sliced, hot or cold, plain or with a pudding sauce or whipped cream.

Cheese Straws

1 cup cake flour	1 cup grated highly flavored
⅛ teaspoon salt	American cheese
Few grains cayenne	3 tablespoons Nucoa
	1 egg yolk

Put the flour, seasonings and cheese in a bowl. Rub in the Nucoa and the egg yolk, mixed with two tablespoons cold water. The mixture should be stiff enough to hold together. Roll to one-eighth inch thickness; and cut into strips about five inches long and one-fourth inch wide. Twist these. Lay the strips on a slightly floured baking sheet; and bake carefully in a moderate oven, 350 degrees F., until crisp. This makes about one and a half dozen.

CANDIES

The newest baby is being christened in a little French Mediterranean town, and all the friends and neighbors are bringing their gifts—boxes, bowls and paper sacks filled with dragées. These sugar-coated nuts and fruits are a traditional part of the ceremony, and no self-respecting baby would consider himself properly christened without them.

Candies and sugar plums are good-will offerings the world over! The guest bearing sweets is always welcome. But how much more welcome when the candies are the real home-made kind!

That's not hard—nor expensive—if you choose the newest ingredients—the New Nucoa, for instance, as used by the best confectioners. Candies containing it have a smoothness of texture and a fineness of flavor commonly associated with expensive brands—a luxury flavor at an economy cost.

ALL MEASUREMENTS ARE LEVEL

French Chocolate Creams

2 cups granulated sugar	2½ tablespoons Nucoa
1 cup cream	1 teaspoon vanilla
⅛ teaspoon salt	½ pound dipping chocolate

Combine the sugar, cream and salt; and stir until the sugar has dissolved. Boil at a moderate rate to 238 degrees F. by a candy thermometer, or until a little when dropped in cold water forms a soft ball. Add the Nucoa and vanilla; turn onto a large platter or marble slab rubbed with Nucoa and cool slightly. Beat with a large spoon or spatula until the mixture is creamy; then knead and form into small balls the size of marbles. Set aside for several hours to chill and dry. Melt the dipping chocolate in the top of a double boiler; remove from the heat and cool to room temperature; using a long-handled fork or spoon, dip the centers in the melted chocolate. Drain; and place on waxed paper until the coating hardens.

92

Creamy Chocolate Fudge

2½ squares (ounces) chocolate   ¼ teaspoon salt
2 cups granulated sugar   ½ cup top cream
½ cup white corn syrup   2 tablespoons Nucoa
1 teaspoon vanilla

Cut the chocolate in bits and combine with the sugar, corn syrup, salt, top cream and Nucoa. Cook and stir the mixture over a moderate heat until boiling point is reached and the sugar has dissolved. Then continue to cook without stirring, to 238 degrees F. by a candy thermometer, or until a little when tried in cold water forms a soft ball. Remove from the heat and cool until tepid. Add the vanilla; and beat until thick and creamy. Transfer to a shallow pan, rubbed lightly with Nucoa, and cool. When almost cold mark in squares.

Vanilla Caramels

½ cup white corn syrup   ¾ cup top cream or undiluted
1 cup granulated sugar   evaporated milk
1½ cups brown sugar   1 tablespoon vanilla
½ cup honey   1 cup heavy cream
⅓ cup Nucoa   A few grains salt

Combine the corn syrup, sugars, honey, Nucoa, top cream and vanilla; and cook over a moderate heat until boiling point is reached. Then stir in the heavy cream and salt; and cook to 254 degrees F. by a candy thermometer, or until a chewy ball results when a little is tried in cold water. Beat until thick and creamy. Transfer to a bread pan rubbed with Nucoa, making the mixture one-half inch deep. When firm remove from the pan, cut in squares, and wrap in waxed paper.

Nut Caramels

Follow the preceding recipe for vanilla caramels, adding three-fourths cup coarsely chopped walnuts to the mixture, after removing it from the heat.

Quick Fondant

½ cup Nucoa   2 teaspoons vanilla
2 cups sifted confectioners' sugar   Vegetable coloring (optional)

Cream the Nucoa until soft and light. Gradually work in the sugar and vanilla and mix until well blended. Transfer to a board or platter dusted with confectioners' sugar and knead with the hands for a few minutes. Divide in thirds and color with vegetable coloring, if desired. It is then ready to be used as a foundation for bonbons, a stuffing for fruits, etc.

Bonbons

Make the Quick Fondant as directed in the preceding recipe. Flavor and color as desired. Form into small balls about the size of a marble; roll in chocolate sprinkles, in plain shredded or toasted coconut, finely chopped pistachio nuts, or toasted almonds, or in confectioners' or granulated sugar. Transfer to a shallow pan lined with waxed paper; and set aside for several hours to ripen and dry out.

Stuffed Fruits

Follow the recipe for Quick Fondant, flavoring it with a little grated orange rind. If dates are used, remove the pits. Slit open moist figs; and soak, drain and pit prunes. Fill with the fondant. Roll in granulated sugar and set aside for several hours to ripen.

Taffy

1 cup molasses	¼ cup cold water
1 cup sugar	2 tablespoons Nucoa
1 teaspoon vinegar	1 teaspoon vanilla
A few grains soda	

Combine the molasses, sugar and vinegar; add one-fourth cup water; and cook together over a moderate heat to 250 degrees F. by a candy thermometer, or until a little when tried in cold water rattles against the side of the cup. Add the Nucoa, vanilla and soda. Transfer to a shallow pan rubbed with Nucoa. Cool, and when almost cold mark in squares.

Salted Nuts

Shell the nuts. Cover with cold water, bring to boiling point, drain and rub off the skins. Melt some Nucoa and pour over the nuts so that each is coated with it. Place in a shallow pan and bake until a delicate brown in a hot oven, 375-400 degrees F. Drain on crumpled paper towels, sprinkle sparingly with salt and cool.

INDEX

95